Entrepreneur MAGAZINE'S

ULTIMATE BOOK OF BUSINESS LETTERS

Customize Your Letters, Memos,
E-mails and Presentations
with the Enclosed CD-ROM

CHERYL KIMBALL and JONI VAN GELDER

EP
Entrepreneur. Press

Editorial Director: Jere Calmes

Acquisitions Editor: Karen Thomas

Cover Design: Beth Hansen-Winter

Production and Editorial Services: CWL Publishing Enterprises, Inc., Madison, Wisconsin, www.cwlpub.com.

This publication is designed to provide accurate and authoritative information in regard to the subject matter covered. It is sold with the understanding that the publisher is not engaged in rendering legal, accounting, or other professional services. If legal advice or other expert assistance is required, the services of a competent professional person should be sought.

> —From a Declaration of Principles jointly adopted by
> a Committee of the American Bar Association and
> a Committee of Publishers and Associations

ISBN 13: 978-19-3253176-3
Printed in Canada

Library of Congress Cataloging-in-Publication Data

Kimball, Cheryl.
   Ultimate book of business letters : customize your letters, memos, e-mails and presentations with the enclosed CD-ROM / by Cheryl Kimball and Joni van Gelder.
      p. cm.
   ISBN 13: 978-19-3253176-3
   ISBN 10: 1-932531-76-9 (alk. paper)
   1. Commercial correspondence. 2. Form letters. I. van Gelder, Joni. II. Title.
HF5721.K54 2007
651.7'5--dc22

                                                        2006023934

11 10 09 08 07 06   10 9 8 7 6 5 4 3 2 1

Contents

Preface

The purpose of this book is to make you a better letter/memo/e-mail/fax writer. It provides guidelines and principles for each type of written business communication you're likely to encounter in your worklife. Written communication varies depending on purpose, recipient, context, and situation. If your letter or memo has the wrong tone, you might not get the response you're looking for.

In verbal communication, well over half of your meaning comes from body language, tone of voice, and words chosen. In written communication, meaning is also derived from more than the words that appear on paper. Some situations require formality, others are informal. Some recipients may know a lot about the context of the communication; others have little background on what you're writing about. Ultimately this book will teach you to effectively get your point across in every type of business situation.

Part 1 provides an overview of the basic principles of written business communication, with one chapter each devoted to style, letters, memos, faxes, and e-mail. In each chapter, we provide guidelines for using these forms of written communication along with selected examples. You may think you know these principles already, but it's still a good review, and we think you might find a few nuggets that will help you improve the quality of your written messages, regardless of the medium you choose.

Parts 2 and 3 form the heart of this book. These parts include model letters you can use or adapt for your particular business.

Part 2 contains letters for start-up. It includes three chapters on seeking information to help write your business plan, seeking information to help with your marketing plan, and how to write to different people when seeking funding for your business. Each chapter includes numerous example letters, nearly all of which include margin explanations of the hows and whys of the letter on that page.

Part 3 is the longest part and provides guidance on letters for all operations while also supplying a quick review of previously discussed contents. You'll find 10 to 20 models in each of these chapters that you can use and adapt.

In addition to the letters in this book, the accompanying CD includes all those in the book plus hundreds more that you can load onto your computer and adapt as appropriate. This disk will save you hours of time in not having to reinvent the wheel to communicate with outsiders, suppliers, customers, employees, and others in your everyday worklife.

Part 1

Basics of Business Communication and Protocol

Introduction

Write a letter? In the e-mail age? An outdated concept? Think again.

Letter writing may be the exception in much day-to-day correspondence, but it is still as important to conducting business as it was in the pre-email era. Written letters provide many benefits:

- Written letters are still the best documentation. A letter sent with some form of delivery confirmation is still the best way to prove you communicated with whomever you are trying to communicate with. Sometimes a letter is a legal necessity.

- Written letters are more private and secure than e-mail. Oh, sure, the secretary or your assistant can read a letter. But that is a lot different from an e-mail, which can accidentally, intentionally, or deviously be broadcast to millions.

- Written letters are without a doubt more professional than e-mail. E-mail is intended to be a quick way to communicate something that's not critical.

- E-mails are more immediate, yes, but you can always fax a letter if the contents aren't confidential or, if they are, send it overnight, which is still pretty darn fast. If something is important enough to be communicated faster than by overnight mail, you might want to pick up the phone—and follow up with a letter.

- A letter can be a critical component of a marketing campaign. In a letter you can take the time you need to support the marketing materials enclosed in the package.

- Even if the correspondence is in-house, a written memo is important in many cases.

1

Other Choices

Sometimes a letter is not the right choice. For instance:

- If you want something that can be posted on a bulletin board at its final destination, a flyer might be the better way to go—few people want to stand at a bulletin board and read a letter. You will need to get your message across in bulleted lists and short paragraphs that can be boxed and printed in larger type. A flyer will cost more than a letter, since you will probably need to have it printed by an offset printer in order to use attractive graphics.

- If you want something to be printed in a publication, the best route is a formal press release. While the press release may sound much like a letter, newspaper and magazine editors will expect the piece to be in the form of a press release. You will need to use the specific conventions of press releases.

- If you want to include a coupon or an application form, you may want to create a something like a trifold brochure. This allows you to include quite a lot of information and also set up one of the flaps so the recipient can clip it and send it back as an application or coupon. Again, you will probably need to consider the additional expense of an offset printer for this, depending on the quantity you plan to do, your publishing software, and the quality of your office printer.

Letters as E-Mail Attachments

Sometimes e-mail is the best way to send a letter. But send the letter as an attachment to the e-mail, not as an insertion. An attachment is a much more formal document, the recipient can print it out without any e-mail text, and the printed document will look just like a letter.

Never, however, send your letter as an attachment without including a note in the e-mail indicating you are sending an attachment and specifying the subject of the letter. Some office firewalls block attachments unless the sender is on a list that allows attachments from his or her e-mail address. If you do not include a note about the attachment and the subject, you may get rejected by a "human firewall": sometimes people automatically trash e-mail attachments that arrive without a personal note, since there are viruses that use e-mail lists to spread as attachments to e-mails that arrive with the From: address of colleagues or friends, so the recipients open the attachment and their computers are immediately infected with the virus. So somehow alert your recipient that you are sending an e-mail with an attachment.

One of the best ways to write effective business letters is to be extremely comfortable with your material. Once you get the hang of it, you will enjoy writing letters instead of dreading it.

Five Steps to Planning Any Business Letter

1. Decide what you are hoping to accomplish with the letter.
2. Determine the best person to whom you should address the letter.
3. Get to the point as efficiently as possible. Don't bury it within so much text that the reader tosses the letter in the trash without reaching the point.

4. If you can use a bulleted list, do so. It breaks up the text and makes the reader more inclined to at least skim the entire letter.

5. Know how you want the reader to respond—and point that out in the letter.

When Is a Letter Better?

Sometimes e-mails, faxes, memos, or even phone calls work great for conducting business. But often a letter can be the best form of communication. Here are ten of those times:

1. You need to come across in a serious way. Letters with a return address, an inside address, a salutation, a closing, and a signature are very official.

2. What you are saying requires your official signature.

3. The contents of the letter will serve as legal documentation; e.g., you are giving someone a warning about his or her job performance.

4. You want the contents to be private. Of course, the recipient can choose to share the letter, but privacy can be lost accidentally more easily with e-mail and faxes.

5. You want to be formal. Your choice of words and tone will probably always be more formal in a letter. Faxes are by nature cryptic and e-mails are by nature informal.

6. You want your communication to be easily retrievable. Although a letter may not be as formal as legal documentation, a letter can be easily filed and readily accessed later if necessary.

7. Letters can make the recipient feel very special. In our fast-paced society where we can communicate instantly and globally with ease, a letter still says, "This was written especially for you"—even if you've sent out a mass mailing of thousands of them!

8. You would like a letter in reply. Sending a letter can convey the expectation that you expect a letter in return.

9. You've tried other means of communication to no avail. Sometimes you've attempted to get across your message in a phone conversation, but the person just isn't hearing it. Or you've sent an e-mail, but gotten no response. A letter, especially if sent by certified mail, will capture the attention of the recipient, who will probably read it closely and now get your message.

10. You want the recipient to carefully consider the information you are providing. How many times have you read an e-mail and realized later that you'd missed some key points? A letter encourages the recipient to read as slowly as the message requires and go over each point to make sure he or she understands it.

Keep file folders on your computer of all the letters you write, even if you use the templates in this book or on the enclosed CD. You will be tailoring them to suit your situations and you can use a lot of the same language again and again.

TIP

The Legal Side of Letter Writing

There is probably not a thing you commit to print that you shouldn't expect could someday become public, intentionally or by accident, or be subpoenaed as evidence in court. Keep that possibility in mind when communicating in writing (electronically or on paper). Few people are going to go to the time, trouble, and expense to tape record phone conversations; besides, there are some laws against taping people without their knowledge and the use of such tapes is often inadmissible in court.

If you have any inkling that a letter spells potential legal trouble, have it read by a lawyer. It just isn't worth taking the chance. You should definitely get legal help with the following letters:

- Letters terminating employees
- Letters reprimanding employees
- Letters responding to lawsuit threats
- Letters responding to safety complaints about your product, service, or business
- Letters responding to employees or former employees involving or alleging sexual harassment or discrimination of any kind

Delivery Options

A letter can be your most effective means of communication—but only if the intended recipient actually receives the letter! You need to choose the most appropriate delivery method. Your options include the United States Postal Service (USPS), Federal Express (FedEx), United Parcel Service (UPS or "Brown"), and smaller delivery services, such as DHL.

Your choice may sometimes depend simply on where your letter is headed. You may have already set up an account with a delivery service because that service is the most logical choice for most of the things you send out. You can certainly use any one of the other delivery services for any individual need; you just won't get the good rate that you probably negotiated with your usual service.

Federal Express and many other delivery services offer not only next-day service but also your choice of morning (priority overnight) or afternoon (regular overnight). There are two things to keep in mind about spending the extra money for priority service. (You didn't think it was a free choice, did you?)

- Many times, especially in larger cities, the overnight delivery arrives in the morning anyway.
- If you want morning delivery, you should check to be sure that the recipient's area even gets this service. This is especially true for rural areas and often for home deliveries.

The lesson is that if you want priority overnight service and enough to pay extra, just make sure you will actually get the service.

CAUTION

## Chapter 1

Business Letter Style

There are two kinds of business letter style: the standard style and your style. Your letters should be a mix of both. You want to make sure to follow the conventions of good business letter writing, including format. And you want your letters to sound like you.

But before you even get to that point, there are some important things to keep in mind as you write letters. These are the good old standard rules that you should follow for any letter worth the paper.

Accuracy

Accuracy in both your facts and your presentation is key to making sure your readers take your letters seriously. While you should always check all facts and the spelling of every word, you should be most attentive to the following items:

- *Recipient name.* Few things turn a reader off more surely than his or her name spelled wrong. Or being titled Mr. when you are a Ms. or being titled Mrs. when you are a Ms. or Mr. If you are using a huge mailing list, you are at the mercy of your list provider. However, if you are creating a mailing list through your business (and if you aren't, you should be!), use every opportunity to double-check the list. If the client visits or calls your business and you haven't seen him or her in a while, politely ask for permission to check his or her listing in your database.

- *Recipient address.* This is important to verify when you have the client on the phone or in front of you. While some letters and packages still get to their intended destination despite some astonishing address misspellings, it doesn't say much for your business when the recipient pulls something out of the mailbox addressed to "Dilver Street" instead of "Silver Street." When something is returned as undeliverable, be sure to update your mailing list as soon as possible—and definitely before you send another mailing of any kind. It may even be worth phoning the customer to get the correct address. Postage is high enough these days to make a call cost-effective.

- *Headlines.* If your letter or flyer has headlines in large type, check and double-check them. We commonly overlook mistakes in headlines because we read what we expect them to say. This is a glaring way for your letter or flyer to impress recipients–negatively.

- *Boxed material.* The same goes for text in boxes or otherwise highlighted: double-check the information and the words and then have someone not involved in the project read them.

- *Your business name.* Unless the business name is imprinted on the piece, check it! It is the utmost of sloppiness to spell your own business name wrong. And people will notice!

Then there are the facts. Before you even sit down to write the letter, gather any facts, figures, statistics, etc. that you plan to use in your letter. As you do this, keep notes on your sources. If you call people and ask questions to gather information, note their name, the company they work for, their position at the company, and their contact information and then keep it all on file. If you need to back up your facts or recheck their accuracy, you'll know exactly where you got them. Do the same if you find information on the Internet or in a book. Make note of the URL or the title of the book, the author, the publisher, the ISBN, and the copyright date and where you found the book so you can get back to it easily.

Grammar

This is where you will wish you'd paid more attention in those boring high school English classes that focused on grammar. You won't need to diagram any sentences, but if you want to look and sound professional, you will do yourself a favor by brushing up on your grammar skills.

There are numerous books that can wait patiently by your side and provide all the help you need as you write and rewrite your letters. These are a few of those "assistants":

- *The Elements of Style* by William Strunk, Jr., and E.B. White. Known informally as "Strunk & White," this succinct little book on grammar and style issues is well worth the shelf space. While it is not an easy reference book, if you thumb through it you will find all of those grammatical details that have plagued you all of your life–like the difference between *affect* and *effect,* the proper use of "fewer" and "less," and how to form possessives and plurals–and a section on style. While the book is not focused specifically on business writing and some of the style tips may be counter to what is considered effective marketing copy, you should keep this book at your side.

- *Merriam-Webster's Collegiate Dictionary.* This is the dictionary most commonly used in publishing circles and it will suit your needs well. The latest edition as of this writing is the 11th. Now that is a moot point, as you can use the online version (www.m-w.com) for free. There are other dictionaries (including some published by Merriam-Webster) that you can also download from a CD to your computer and use when you are not online. Don't hesitate to use this incredible tool, either to check spelling or to confirm the meaning of a word. It takes only a second to make sure— and accuracy is critical to the credibility of your letters.

- *The Chicago Manual of Style.* This book is almost an institution in itself, the bible of all copy editors and proofreaders. Although the organization is a little confusing, once you get the hang of it you will be amazed by how you can find almost every point of grammar and usage in this comprehensive book. You might find another style manual that works better for you, such as *The Associated Press Style Book* or *Words into Type.* Pick the one that works for you or use the one that is standard for your audience—and then be consistent. Customers will notice.

Grammar Pitfalls to Avoid

You don't have to be a grammar genius to write good letters, but you do need to avoid the most common grammar pitfalls that make you look less polished. These include the following:

- Use "between" only with two items and "among" with three or more. For example, "She sat among five strangers" and "She sat between two strangers."
- "Me" is an object and "I" is a subject. For example, "You and I are going" and "A package came for you and me." A good way to check your usage of these pronouns is to drop the other person from the sentence and see if it sounds right. For the above examples, "Me am going" wouldn't sound right, nor would "A package came for I."
- Learn the difference between "affect" and "effect." According to our friend Merriam-Webster, "affect" is a transitive verb and means "to act upon."; if you could use "touch" or "influence" or "change" as the verb in your sentence instead of "affect," then "affect" is correct—e.g., "Inflation affects us all" or "Inflation touches/influences/changes us all." "Effect" is a noun or a transitive verb. As a noun, it is defined as a result or an outcome; if you could use "result" or "outcome" as the noun in your sentence instead of "effect," then "effect" is correct—e.g., "That was the effect he wanted" or "That was the result/outcome he wanted." As a verb, "effect" is defined "to cause to come into being"; if you could use "cause" as the verb in your sentence instead of "effect," then "effect" is correct—e.g., "She effected a change" or "She caused a change."
- Learn how to use apostrophes correctly. The main two uses of apostrophes are for possessives and contractions. We use an apostrophe to show possession with nouns, but not with pronouns; with pronouns, an apostrophe indicates a contraction. The biggest problem is "its." So, for example, "the company's assets" but "its assets." Strunk and White give the example of "It's a wise dog that scratches its own fleas." The first "It's" can be read "it is" but the second cannot. If you wonder about using an apostrophe in a word, try saying the word as two words; if you can, it's a contraction and an apostrophe is correct.
- Commas are an issue for even the most experienced copy editors. A good rule of thumb is to keep commas to a minimum! That said, always use a comma for a pause or if it makes a sentence more clear.

In Style

You know the general language style of the business you are in. You talk in that style with colleagues on the phone. Use that same language style in your business letters. However, some letters require that you be a little more formal than others. Adjust to fit the situation.

The best way to develop your business letter writing style is to get writing! Here are some suggestions to keep in mind:

- Keep your letters simple. Use short sentences that are clear and concise. Don't use flowery language and big words just to sound smart—you won't sound smart because you will lose or frustrate your reader. Unless you are writing a letter trying to convince people to take your class on how to write with big words, leave those words in the dictionary.

- Know your target audience and write to those people. Female executives will expect different language than male personal trainers, for example. You don't have to go to extremes, but you should make readers feel that the letter was written to them.

- Convey credibility. Use terms appropriate for the industry. Cite sources for any statistics you use. Include quotes from credible business owners or other respected people in the industry (with their permission, of course). Be precise.

- Be accurate! Check your facts. Have someone else, even more than one person, read your letters before you send them. If you are promising something that will be delivered by another department, check with that department head to be sure you are conveying the right message.

- Finally, put your personality into your letters! People reading letters like to know that a real person is behind the letters and the only way to get that across is to sound like you.

Nine Tips for Effective Business Writing

1. Outline what you want to convey in your letter before you start writing.
2. Once you have decided on your main message, stick to it. People don't have time to read your meanderings; they will just stop reading.
3. Use bulleted and numbered lists to help break up the text and make it easier to read. Big blocks of text look daunting.
4. Start off lively. "Lively" doesn't need to be cute or silly. But don't bore readers with the first sentence. Pick the most interesting fact you found and lead with that.
5. Don't make any promises you can't fulfill—for goods, services, turnaround time, or anything else.
6. Check your facts, check your spelling, and then recheck everything.
7. Have someone read your letter. If the letter is a marketing tool, find a member of your target audience. Also, have your reader question facts and spelling while reading it.
8. Personally sign the letter if at all possible. If you're mailing 10,000 letters, then of course that's not possible. But if it's just 25, get out your best pen and practice your autograph.
9. Lastly, send the letter to the right people.

Proofreading Pitfalls to Avoid

- Don't rely on your computer spell-checker! Certainly use it, but consider it the first-round pass. Remember that a word that is spelled correctly may still be the wrong word! Sum words mite out smart yore soft wear.
- Watch for word choice errors. Some of the most common ones are "they're," "their," and "there" and, as mentioned earlier, the uses of "effect" and "affect."
- Keep a good dictionary on your bookshelf (and on your computer too, if you want). A good thesaurus is also not a bad idea—even the best writers have a block here and there searching for the right word.
- Don't use "ain't" and other grammatically incorrect words just to sound casual. In a letter, such attempts at sounding casual usually will fail and simply sound stupid and demeaning to your reader.

## Chapter 2

Business Letter Basics

Letterhead

In short—get some. With the ease of computer software, you don't even need to get any printed, especially if your business is small, with fewer than a half-dozen employees. A color printer allows you to create letterhead as you write letters.

Word processing programs such as Microsoft Word get more and more sophisticated with every new version. You can use their publishing features or programs to create a letter-head that you save as a template file; every time you want to write a letter, call up that file and create your letter on the template. Most of these programs automatically copy the lower part of the letterhead (usually the address area) to new pages as you write and numbers those pages. Keep a supply of nice stationery on hand for printing your letters.

Like anything else in marketing your business, decide on a color scheme and a typeface for your letterhead and stick with them. Likewise for your stationery color. When customers and clients get a letter on gray stationery with dark purple type for the letterhead, they will start to associate it with your business.

> No matter what color your stationery or what type for your letterhead, print the text of your letters in black. Black ink is cheaper and often comes in bigger cartridges. And it is always easier to read. If you break this rule once in a while for effect, do not print any text in yellow; it is almost always unreadable.

TIP

Format

There is a very simple format to follow for most business letters. Be sure to use it. If you want to be more casual in the body of the letter, that's fine, but keep the letter's appearance formal and neat. It is the best impression to make on all customers you contact by letter.

The examples at the end of this chapter show the actual format. These are the basics:

- *Date, upper left corner.* This seems like a no-brainer, but it's easy to forget to include the date. You want to make sure recipients of your letters know exactly when it was written. And if they file a letter away for future reference, they will know at a glance when the letter was written.

- *Recipient's name, upper left corner in line with the date.* Use the appropriate title. For men, "Mr." is always appropriate, unless the person is an elected official or merits an honorific title, such as "Reverend." For women, always use "Ms." unless you know for certain that the person prefers "Miss" or "Mrs." or she is an elected official or merits an honorific title. And again, make sure to spell the recipient's name correctly—even the simplest names can have alternate spellings.

- *Recipient's address, upper left corner below the name.* Be sure to use the correct address, that you spell street names and cities or towns correctly, and that the ZIP code is correct. First, this is good public relations with the recipient. Second, either a mail merge program or a person addressing envelopes or labels will likely use this address on the envelope—you want to be sure the letter gets to where you want it to go.

- *Closing, flush left, one line space after the body ends.* Keep it simple. "Sincerely" is the most common and probably the best closing to use, especially for letters to people you don't know. Others include "Cordially," "Regards," "Respectfully," "All the best," and "Most sincerely."

- *Signature space, three or four line spaces below the closing.* Leave enough room to sign the letter. A hand-signed letter says a lot. If you are sending a mass mailing and someone is going to stamp your signature, fine, but allow space for it. If you are trying to limit the letter to one page and need to squeeze out a line or two, this is a place to steal a little space.

- *Your name, flush left, below the signature space.* Type your name, no matter how legible your signature. People want to be sure they have the correct spelling of your name.

- *Your title, flush left, directly below your name.* Type the title you hold at your company. This is one of the most important parts of the business letter—the recipient definitely wants to know from what layer of bureaucracy in your company the letter has come.

The Paperless Office?

When computers started to appear on every desktop in businesses across the nation and around the world, there was great chatter about the paperless office. Like the Y2K scare and the end of the printed book, our offices are not paperless and are unlikely to become so in any near future. We like paper. We like things to be printed on paper, for various reasons—it is easier to read, we can make notes on it, paper makes a document seem more real. File cabinets will not be obsolete any time soon.

Nonetheless, some documents can be kept electronically, especially if your office has developed a simple backup system. If your business is big enough, an IT department will be doing backup on your company server on a daily basis. These backups are archived, so any document saved electronically can be accessed, if necessary, although it may not be easy.

On a smaller scale, you can keep a backup of your letters fairly easily. Create an electronic folder that is titled "Letters" with the year, e.g., "Letters 2007." If you write a lot of letters, create a folder for each month. At the end of each week (or daily, if it makes you feel better), save this file to a jump drive or some other portable storage device. Not only does this give you the backup you need, but you can tote that device with you if you work on a laptop outside the office.

There are many ways to do this. For example, you can save the Letters file and e-mail it to your laptop every week and use that as your backup storage. Choose a system that works for you. And then use it.

Letters can be recycled time and again. Call up the Letters file, find a letter that best matches your current need, and change the pertinent information. Then proofread it carefully—you want to avoid leaving any traces from the old letter!

Some Examples

[Date]

[Name]
[Company]
[Address]
[City, State ZIP]

Dear [Mr. or Ms. + Last Name]:

I appreciate your inquiry as to whether my business is for sale. At this time, I am not interested in selling. However, I will certainly keep your inquiry on file in case the time comes that I do decide to sell.

I wish you the best of luck in your search for a business to purchase.

[Closing],

[Your Name]
[Your Title]

Getting an unsolicited inquiry about buying your business can be flattering. Even if you never ever plan to sell your business, don't burn this bridge! Send a thank-you note. Don't just tell the interested party that you will keep his or her name on file—do it! You never know when your personal situation may change and you may decide that it's best to sell your business.

[Date]

[Name]
[Company]
[Address]
[City, State ZIP]

Dear [Mr. or Ms. + Last Name]:

Thank you very much for thinking of a tour of [Your Business Name] as a possible field trip for your students. We do welcome student tours and we enjoy them.

Since we are a small company, we need to limit the number of student tours we conduct each year. Unfortunately, we have already conducted our limit for this school year. If, however, you want to plan one for next year, please contact us when the school year starts in the fall and we will be pleased to try to fit your class into our schedule. The person you should contact is [Name], who arranges all the tours of our plant.

I am sending some information about our company and a box of imprinted pencils as a token of our appreciation for your interest in [Your Business Name]. We hope to see you in the future.

[Closing],

[Name]
[Title]

If at all possible, send with your reply something to help people remember your company, especially if your letter will disappoint them. Keeping magnets, pencils, erasers, key chains, or other small items on hand for such situations can be inexpensive public relations.

[Date]

[Name]
[Company]
[Address]
[City, State ZIP]

Dear [Mr. or Ms. + Last Name]:

I am opening a retail store in a neighboring town. I was hoping I might be able to treat you to breakfast some morning in exchange for chatting with you about the retail experiences you have had. If lunch, dinner, or even late afternoon coffee works better for you, that is fine too.

I will call you next week to see if there is a good time for us to meet.

Thanks very much.

[Closing],

[Name]
[Business/Title, if Appropriate]

Although this kind of query could also be done by phone, it is often best to introduce yourself by letter and give a person a heads-up that you will be calling.

[Date]

[Name]
[Company]
[Address]
[City, State ZIP]

Dear [Mr. or Ms. + Last Name]:

[Your Real Estate Company Name] is always ready to help homeowners sell their homes or land. The market in your area is strong. If you have been thinking about selling, now is a great time.

I have enclosed my business card. I welcome the opportunity to talk with you about how I could make your dreams become reality.

[Closing],

[Name]
[Business Title, if Appropriate]

Avoid the generic "Dear Homeowner" whenever possible. Instead, use names to make the query sound more personal than a global search for properties for sale.

[Date]

[Name]
[Company]
[Address]
[City, State ZIP]

Dear [Mr. or Ms. + Last Name]:

Please allow me to introduce myself as the Director of a new funeral home in your community. [Your Company Name] has been in business in the neighboring town of [Town Name] since 1985. My father started our funeral home and my sister and I run it. We are proud of our years of service to the people in the greater [Town Name] area.

[Your Company Name]'s mission is to help families get through a difficult time with the knowledge that someone with our history of experience is taking care of the details.

Please let us know how we can be of service to you. We offer pre-paid funeral plans and can walk you and your family through the options. And you can take comfort in knowing that we understand and we care.

[Closing],

[Your Name]
[Your Title]
[Company Name]

Always include your business card with every letter you send to someone new.

[Date]

[Name]
[Company]
[Address]
[City, State ZIP]

Dear [Mr. or Ms. + Last Name]:

I am so excited to announce my new pet-sitting service in the greater [City Name] area! [Your Business Name] promises to offer the highest-quality care. You can count on your pet being well cared for, while you are away on a long weekend retreat or off on a business trip or just at work for the day.

I am a licensed veterinary technician and worked in a veterinarian's office for the past five years. My dog, Sal, and my cat, Rainbow, will attest to the great care I give animals!

The enclosed flyer outlines the services I offer. I look forward to meeting your pets and caring for them in the near future.

[Closing],

[Your Name]
[Your Business Name]

Keep your letter simple, friendly, low-key, and uncluttered. Enclose your brochure of services and let it do the work you designed it to do!

[Date]

[Name]
[Company]
[Address]
[City, State ZIP]

Dear [Mr. or Ms. + Last Name]:

We are pleased to have been selected by the town of [Town Name] to be your new recycling service company.

[Your Business Name] has been the business of recycling for over 30 years. Our mission is to provide you with quality service and to make it easy for you to recycle. We will do curbside pickup of glass, plastic, paper, and cardboard.

The enclosed flyer should cover everything you need to know to get your recyclables ready for us to pick up on Tuesday mornings, beginning [Date]. If you still have questions, we encourage you to call at 888-555-5555.

We look forward to many years of serving you and your town.

[Closing],

[Company President Name], President
[Company name]

Start off every new relationship with a friendly welcoming letter. Always repeat your phone number—even if it is already on the letterhead and the flyer—so customers don't feel they have to search for it.

[Date]
[Name]
[Company]
[Address]
[City, State ZIP]

Dear [Mr. or Ms. + Last Name]:

I am pleased to announce that your building has a new supervisor. Her name is [Name] and she can be reached at [Phone Number].

[Name] has many years of experience as building supervisor for a large apartment complex in [City Name]. She comes to us highly recommended by both her previous employer and several tenants in the buildings under her care.

In order to start getting to know you and to introduce herself, [Name] will be present at the next building meeting on May 1st. Please try to stop by and meet [Name]. [Company Name] will be providing refreshments at the meeting to encourage you to linger and chat with [Name] and welcome her to the building.

[Closing],

[Name]
[Company]

Introductions of new people are important business letters to write. They don't have to be long and involved, just enough need-to-know information to let customers know that you have tried to keep their needs in mind by hiring the right people.

[Date]

[Name]
[Company]
[Address]
[City, State ZIP]

Dear [Mr. or Ms. + Last Name]:

[Store Name] will again this year be taking donations for the annual Toys for Tots drive. Our customers have always been extremely generous to children in need over the holiday season and we look forward to making this another record-breaking year!

For every 20 toys collected, [Store Name] will donate one tricycle from our inventory.

The collection van will be in our parking lot from November 1 through December 10. Please stop by during our business hours (Monday through Saturday 9-6, Sunday 12-5) to drop off your donations of

---

unwrapped new toys. All donors are invited to come in and fill out a raffle ticket to enter to win some great prizes donated by other local businesses.

[Business Name] takes great pleasure in doing this for our kids and we thank you for your generosity.

[Closing],

[Your Name]
[Company Name]

A charitable cause is always a good opportunity to send a friendly letter to your customers. Do it early enough to allow them sufficient time to participate.

[Date]
[Name]
[Company]
[Address]
[City, State ZIP]

Dear [Mr. or Ms. + Last Name]:

[Business Name] is delighted to let you know we have hired a new caregiver in the toddler area of our day care center.

[Name] is a former kindergarten teacher and mother of two pre-teens. We know you will welcome her to our staff. And we are pleased to announce that with the arrival of [Name] we now are able to open up two more places in our toddler section. If you know of families looking for quality day care for their toddler, we would appreciate your recommendation.

Thanks for your continued support, and please say "hello" to [Name] when you come to pick up your child.

[Closing],

[Name]
[Business]

In a child-care situation, you can take the opportunity of announcing a new hire to solicit new business.

## Chapter 3

Memo Basics

The memo—short for "memorandum" (plural, "memoranda")—is typically an in-house document. In fact, Merriam-Webster's definition is "a usually brief informal communication typically written for interoffice circulation." The memo is used to make announcements such as policy changes, hirings, or promotions; to serve as reminders of policy or regulations or an upcoming event; or to provide general information to employees.

Memos can be company-wide or intradepartmental. They can also be interdepartmental, whether the information in the memo needs to be exchanged only between two departments or among more.

Format

Memo format is fairly simple. Some companies have stationery or a digital template with MEMORANDUM printed at the top. If so, you can delete the word "memo" from the first two items in the following format. Otherwise, at the top of the page you need the following six items:

- Memo to: Specify the intended recipients—an individual, a group of employees, or the entire company

- Memo from: People reading the memo should be told who sent it. Indicate your title and/or department. Unless your company is very small, don't assume people know your first and last name.

- Date: Always date every written correspondence, even the simplest memo.

- RE: This is the reason for the memo. Keep it short—a few words or a short phrase. The RE: line should not rival the body of the memo.

- Pages: Always indicate the number of pages. If the memo is longer than one page, number each page (1 of 3, 2 of 3, etc.).

- Extenuating information: Indicate if the memo is confidential—i.e., the information is not intended to leave the company. Keep in mind that, however you label them, memos can easily end up in outside hands, often simply by accident.

The Body of the Memo

Keep memos brief and to the point. It is not necessary to be chatty or conversational. You don't really even have to use complete sentences, although it is always better to do that if space allows for it.

Use normal punctuation and paragraphing. You do not need to sign a memo at the bottom in a letter-style signature space, although you may want to put your signature beside your name at the top, especially if the information in the memo is of the sort that people might question the authenticity or the authority of the memo (such as for an announcement of changes in a dress code, for example).

Accuracy

As with all written correspondence, have someone else read the memo before you send it out. Pick someone who is a good proofreader and has good grammatical skills. Accuracy in any correspondence, in-house or not, is an important part of portraying an image of credibility and professionalism.

> If you are the boss or the owner, be sure your written correspondence is as well written and accurate as you expect your employees' correspondence reflecting your company to be.

TIP

MEMO TO: All Employees
MEMO FROM: The Management Committee
DATE: May 15, 2006
RE: Summer Hours
# of pages (including this one): one

The Management Committee is pleased to announce summer hours, commencing the week of June 5 and ending the week of August 28. As in the past, each employee is welcome to pick whichever half day (four hours) during the week he or she would like to have free and make up for it by working an extra hour each of the other four days. Please keep in mind the following guidelines:

- The half day you pick can't change each week; you need to stick to the same half day all summer.
- Likewise, please pick the times of the other four days when you would like to make up for the free half day and stick with them all summer.
- Be sure to clear your choice with your supervisor. All business hours must be covered in your department, so be sure to have a second choice in case your first choice conflicts with that goal.

We appreciate your cooperation. Enjoy your summer hours!

In-house memos are a common way to impart information to all employees—they can be dropped in everyone's mailbox and posted on a common bulletin board.

MEMORANDUM

TO: All [STORE NAME] Stores
FROM: Corporate Sales Office
DATE: May 18, 2007
RE: Ad correction

Please be advised that the flyer that is being distributed with the Sunday May 28 papers has incorrect information. The Brand-X gas grill is listed as being on sale for $149.95. In fact the sale price is $129.95.

Please post the attached correction sheet near the entrance to your store and in the area where you display grills.

We apologize for the inconvenience.

Use the memo format to pass along a single, important piece of information.

MEMO TO: Jane Doe, Marketing Manager
MEMO FROM: Jane Smith, President
DATE: 4 November 2006
RE: Late employees

I have noticed and other managers have pointed out to me that several employees in your department regularly arrive for work later than the designated 8:30 start time. Please be advised that you need to correct this situation or I will need to take action. Arriving late for work is inconsistent with the work ethic of our company. To not address this situation is unfair to the rest of the employees of the company.

Since you and I have discussed this situation more than once before and you have assured me you would take action, this memo is being recorded in your company file. I am sure you will find a way to correct this by 31 January 2007. If you need management support to take action, please be sure to let me know.

You would not use a memo to point out employee lateness the first time. But in this situation, as noted in the memo, the president and the manager have already discussed this problem more than once. The memo documents the problem in writing in a form that can be filed in the company records for the manager.

MEMO TO: All Employees
FROM: John Jones, Director, Customer Service
DATE: 10 February 2005
RE: Promotion

I am pleased to announce that Ellen Smith has been promoted to Manager, Customer Service.

Ellen has been with [Company Name] for seven years, starting in 1998 as a part-time customer service operator.

In her current role as Assistant Manager, Customer Service, Ellen has implemented several ideas that have significantly increased the efficiency of our customer service operators and provided them with more information to better serve our customers. There were four qualified candidates for this vacancy, but the search committee is confident that Ellen is the best choice for the job at this time.

I know you will join me in congratulating Ellen on this well-deserved promotion.

An in-house promotion is a common use of the memorandum format.

MEMO TO: All Employees
FROM: Allen Smith, Marketing Manager
DATE: 5 April 2007
RE: Visitor

Please be advised that Mr. Chin and Ms. Ming will be visiting us from Aerial Printing in Hong Kong, China, on 12 April.

Our marketing department does a great deal of business with Aerial Printing. We have had a long relationship with Mr. Chin, owner of the company. His associate, Ms. Ming, has been named customer service rep for our company. We are excited to host them at [Company Name] and know that all employees will join us in welcoming them.

For this special visit, we all will want to put on our best company face. There will be a small reception for Mr. Chin and Ms. Ming from 4:30 to 5:00 pm on 12 April in the foyer and all employees are encouraged to attend.

The information in this memo could also be imparted to employees via e-mail. Putting it in a written memo makes it easy to post on company bulletin boards, further ensuring that everyone in the company sees it.

Fax Basics

The facsimile machine, patented by Alexander Bain, a Scottish clockmaker, in 1843, was a natural progression from Samuel Morse's telegraph technology, transmitting images as signals through telegraph wires. The technology developed through the first three-quarters of the 20th century and fax machines became ubiquitous in offices in the 1980s and into the 1990s, before the proliferation of e-mail and electronic ways to scan and transmit images quicker and with higher quality than the fax.

Despite the common use of e-mail, faxes still serve a purpose. Most offices have a scanner and it isn't that complicated or time-consuming to scan images, but it is one more step. With a fax machine, you walk to the machine with your piece of paper, feed it into the machine, dial the number, and press "start." That's all—no need to scan the image first. The quality of the image received by the recipient depends greatly both on the quality of the original and on the quality of the machines at both ends. The quality of fax machines is typically not high enough for today's publication standards. They are, however, just fine for transmitting information, as long as the recipients can read the text and see any images clearly enough.

Fax Marketing

A practice that has become prevalent in the past few years is blanket marketing by fax. When telemarketing proliferated to the point that regulations were established to limit the use of telemarketing and to create the federal "Do Not Call" list, telemarketers needed to find a new way to market to the masses. Faxes became an option.

The value of this option is questionable. The recipients often get annoyed by unsolicited marketing faxes: they are paying for the fax toner and paper that marketers are using to spread their messages—and neither of those is cheap.

The chances are very good that the recipients will toss the fax unread or use it for scrap paper. But there is no easy way for recipients to stop unsolicited faxes. The Telephone

Consumer Protection Act of 1991 (TCPA) is the primary law governing the conduct of telephone solicitation; the TCPA restricts the use of automatic dialing systems, artificial or prerecorded voice messages, and fax machines to send unsolicited advertisements. In 2006, the Federal Communications Commission made changes in the fax advertising rules of the TCPA that, among other things, require the sender of fax ads to provide specified notice and contact information on the fax that allows recipients to opt out of future faxes from the sender. The new rules took effect August 1, 2006.

Still, if companies in your industry have used faxes in marketing with some success, you might want to give it a try.

Just the Fax

Faxes are quite simple. You want to send some information on paper immediately. You write something and then transmit it from your fax machine to another or hundreds of others. The most common faxes are:

- *Very brief.* Typically you are just providing some information to the recipient, which you want him or her to have immediately and in writing.
- *Cover sheets.* Your fax memo is often just a cover sheet for something else you're faxing, such as a magazine article, a price sheet, or a photo.

The Fax Memo

To create a fax cover sheet (which often constitutes the entire fax), you need to put some basic information at the top of the fax. This information is often similar to the information you put at the top of a memo and often in the same style:

- the recipient's name (TO:)
- your name (FROM:)
- the date (DATE:)
- the subject of the fax (RE:)
- the number of pages, including the cover sheet (# of pages including this one:)

Always put page numbers on multipage faxes. If there are many pages, the fax machine on the other end may spit out the pages onto the floor and the recipient will have to figure out the order of the pages. Likewise, as your fax machine sends the multipage fax, the sheets may end up on the floor, so page numbers may help you too.

TIP

When Faxes Are Not Good to Use

When should you not use a fax? Confidential information should rarely if ever be sent by fax. Perhaps if you know for sure that the recipient works in a one-person office and you are 100 percent sure the recipient will be the person picking the fax off the machine, then it's OK. But faxes simply are not private enough to use to send confidential information.

Material containing photos that are critical to the information also are best not faxed. Even the best faxes are not good photo printers. It would be better to photocopy the material on a high-quality copier and send that copy or, if it makes sense, the originals. You can use overnight mail and get the package to its destination pretty quickly.

Of course, you can fax the pages and follow up by mailing photocopies or the original material if you want the recipient to get the information quickly and also get clear photos.

Last, with these things in mind, anything that requires a high-quality presentation should not be sent by fax. The quality just isn't good enough. Unless the recipient has specifically requested a fax, which means he or she understands that the faxed material may not look as nice as the original, then using overnight mail is really your better option.

Some Examples

FAX TO: Mr. Fred Chin, Aerial Printing
FROM: Allen Smith, Marketing Manager, [Company Name]
DATE: 26 February 2007
RE: Printing Quote
# of pages (including this one): 1

Dear Mr. Chin,

How are you? I hope all is well at Aerial Printing.

[Company Name] is getting ready to print the 2006-2007 annual report. We would like a quote for printing 10,000 copies. The report will be 64 pages long, four-color throughout. We would like 12-point glossy cover stock. We can provide a CD by March 25 and would need the report in our hands by July 30.

Please send your print quote to me at your earliest convenience.

Sincerely,

Allen Smith

If a fax is of a more formal nature, you can format it and sign it as you would a regular letter. A more informal fax, such as to a colleague at a sister company, would not need this formality.

FAX TO: Susan Smith, [Position], [Company Name]
FROM: Sam Jones, [Position], [Company Name]
DATE: 2 November 2006
RE: Attached article
# of pages (including this one): 4

Attached is the article concerning the British marketing firm that did the branding campaign for [Company], which I mentioned might be of interest to you. I found the technique and ideas very helpful when I was working on the [Name] project.

Good luck in your campaign!

Cover sheets for faxing articles and other printed pieces are common uses of the fax format.

FAX TO: Ed Jones, [Position], [Company]
FROM: Sue Smith, [Position], [Company]
DATE: [Date]
RE: [Subject]
# of pages (including this one): [Number]

Please mail the materials we discussed on the phone last night to my attention at the following address:

[Company]
[Building/Suite]
[Street]
[City, State ZIP]

I look forward to receiving them.

You could send a request like this by e-mail, of course. But sometimes you want to hand an address to someone who may not have access to a computer, such as mail room staff, or the person on the other end can just ask the mail room staff to pick up the request straight off the fax.

FAX TO: Sue Smith, [Name] Insurance Company
FROM: Ed Frank, [Title], [Company]
DATE: [Date]
RE: [Subject]
# of pages (including this one): [Number]

Attached please find the signed form for the insurance rider. I have put the original with a check in the mail; you should receive it by Friday.

Thank you for taking care of this.

Faxes are great for all sorts of attachments. In this case, in order for the insurance to take effect, the broker needed a signature.

FAX TO: Cathy Jones
FROM: Sylvia
DATE: [Date]
RE: [Subject]
# of pages (including this one): [Number]

Hi Cath,

Please order 60 each of the following and start putting the kits together if you receive the supplies before I get back:

1 ½" ring binders with plastic sleeve for cover insert
Pocket files
Alpha tabs
Plastic pockets (you know, the kind that holds pens, etc.)

I will finish up the covers and print them when I return. I've attached a photo of the binder I saw that I liked.

See you soon!

Sylvia

This fax is correspondence between colleagues of the same company and can be more informal than business-to-business correspondence.

E-Mail Basics

As the use of e-mail increased, it developed a reputation for encouraging sloppiness. E-mails were presumed to not be subject to the same standards as other written correspondence. They have been considered a fast and easy way to communicate, especially for those growing up with instant messaging and text messaging, with a language often rich with acronyms, abbreviations, and other "words."

Don't be led astray. Sure, if you are writing chatty messages to your friends and you don't want to take the time to check your spelling, that isn't a big deal. But if you fall into the habit of not checking your e-mails for spelling and grammar and not caring if you spell names accurately and punctuate appropriately, you will begin to do this with other e-mail messages as well—whether to your buddies or to others.

E-Mail Etiquette

There are some basic e-mail etiquette issues that are important to follow; see below for a few of the most commonly encountered.

One important fact to understand and keep in mind is that e-mails do not come across the same as a voice on the phone. Any written correspondence has the same shortcoming, but when people write e-mails, they often fall into a false sense of being connected with the person to whom they are writing because an e-mail can be almost as immediate as a phone call. But the tone of voice and the ability to explain immediately when you sense that the other person doesn't understand are missing from e-mail. And this can get you in big trouble.

Read each e-mail you write several times before you press "Send." Check for typos that create crucial changes in meaning, such as "can" for "can't." Double-check the name(s) you have entered in the "To" line before you hit "Send." When you pull a name from your address book, it is so easy to get the wrong one.

Here are other things to keep in mind:

- Never send confidential information via e-mail. Once you press "Send," it is too late to take it back, even if you realize you put the wrong person in the "To" line!

- DON'T USE ALL CAPS. In the e-mail world, this is considered "shouting" and offensive.

- If you are responding to one recipient of an e-mail that was sent out to several people, be careful to choose "reply to sender" and not "reply to all." It's annoying to have to weed through messages that are only personal exchanges between two people.

- Reserve the "high priority" label for e-mails that are, in fact, high priority. Labeling as "high priority" e-mails that are not is like the old story of the boy who cried wolf—if you send an e-mail that truly is high priority, your recipients may not believe you.

- Do not encourage, and certainly do not forward, joke e-mails, chain e-mails, and other junk e-mail. Not only does trafficking in junk e-mail convey the impression that you're less than serious about your business, but these e-mails sometimes carry viruses.

- Don't use obscene language in your e-mails. This is just common courtesy.

- Keep attachments to a minimum. Many companies have firewalls that do not allow attachments, so your e-mail may not reach the intended recipient. If you must send an attachment, contact the recipient in advance to make sure he or she can and will accept it.

E-mail has become a critical part of business correspondence. To the extent that e-mail can be used instead of the phone, it can save a lot of money and it can save employee time, since phone calls always entail some chitchat. It is always a good policy to train your employees to use e-mails appropriately to best represent your company.

E-Mail Policy

All companies should have a policy about e-mails. If you own the company, be sure to create a policy and alert all employees to it. If you are an employee, be sure you know company policy and adhere to it. E-mail policies can reduce the possibility of lawsuits over allegations of virus propagation and language and bias issues.

Check and Recheck

When you reread your e-mail before sending it, double- and triple-check the name and address of the recipient. There are many e-mails you would prefer not to send to the wrong person—although you should never put anything in an e-mail would cause a problem if it went beyond the intended recipient. The recipient may forward it without your knowledge or unintentionally. And if you send an e-mail to the wrong person, you may never find out that the intended recipient never received it.

E-mail confirming discussion

> To: Ed Smith
> CC: [Blank]
> Subject: Our conversation
>
> Dear Ed,
>
> Thanks for taking the time last night to discuss the details of your project.
>
> As we discussed you will:
> - review the entire manuscript and return it to me a week from tomorrow
> - put any lengthy editorial additions into a Microsoft Word file, note the pages where they belong, and indicate where in the manuscript to insert the new material
> - include the two missing images in the package
> - rough out what you would like the cover to look like
>
> In the meantime, I will check with the production department to see if the five permissions forms you sent are on file with them.
>
> Thanks, Ed.
>
> Sincerely,
>
> [Your Name]

E-mails are often formatted roughly like a letter, with a salutation, a body, a closing, and a signature block.

Attachment of 5-year sales figures

> To: Sue Smith
> CC: [Blank]
> Subject: Five-year sales of [Product Name]
>
> Dear Ms. Smith:
>
> Attached in a Microsoft Excel file are the 5-year sales figures for the [Product Name]. As you will note, there was a dip in sales during the second quarter of the fourth year while we waited for our manufacturer to renovate their plant. We were able to produce product at an alternative site, but at a slower rate than our main manufacturer.
>
> Please let me know if you need further information. I will call you next week to discuss these figures.
>
> Sincerely,
>
> [Name]
> [Phone]
> [E-Mail Address]

This header format (To, CC, and Subject lines) is used in a popular e-mail program. Other programs may use different formats, such as including a BCC line.

Responding to potential contract

> To: Ed Smith
> CC: [Blank]
> Subject: contract
>
> Dear Mr. Smith:
>
> Thank you for thinking of me regarding the [Name] project. I thought of a couple more things you could send that would help me in estimating how many hours this project might take:
> - the previous version of the report
> - how many products you think it might include
> - if I would be producing the final version and all copies you would need or if you plan to print and collate them at your office
>
> Sincerely,
>
> [Name]
> [Phone]
> [E-Mail Address]

Always include your phone and e-mail address in e-mail correspondence, especially those involving new business. You don't want to obligate the recipient to search for your phone number. If the recipient prints your message, having your e-mail address on it will make it easier to reply, especially if the recipient replies from another computer or asks another person to reply. Finally, if your company has a Web site, you should generally include it, if for no other reason that that a Web site is now considered a business credential.

Finalizing phone conversation time

> To: Sue Jones
> CC: [Blank]
> Subject:
>
> Hi Sue,
>
> I looked at my schedule and the best time of the three you mentioned for our phone conversation is 3 pm Pacific, 6 pm Eastern. I will call you at [Phone Number]. Is this OK?
>
> I look forward to discussing this exciting idea!
>
> Ed

E-mail is a great way to confirm phone appointments. Always be sure to specify time zone (if more than one) and to indicate who will call whom at what number. And be sure to request a response, as e-mails (and voice mails) can end up in never-never land and the person who should have received your message won't be expecting your call.

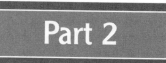

Letters for Start-up

## Chapter 6

Letters Seeking Information for a Business Plan

The start-up phase of any business is exciting and should be full of optimism. You will need to project this optimism in the various types of letters you will need to write for your venture. It's one of the four elements that will be critical to successful start-up letters:

- *Confidence.* If you don't have confidence in your ability to succeed in your venture, no one else will! Your letters need to ooze confidence, although not to the extent that you make readers suspicious. You can easily give the impression of your confidence in your ability and your business category by avoiding phrases and words like "I think," "probably," and other term that make your language less assertive, less emphatic, less positive. For example, instead of saying, "I think there is a strong market in my area for a widget business," say, "There is a strong market …." These little things can make a letter sound very different.

- *Authority.* You want your letters to sound strong and give the impression that you have the ability to take charge of your business. This is especially true for a start-up that is going to involve hiring more than one or two employees. Knowing your industry inside and out will enable you to use the language of the industry and sound like you will have what it takes to make things happen.

- *Credibility.* The way to sound more credible is to point out the parts of your background and experience that make it clear that you are in the know in your industry. You can't establish credibility just in a letter; you need experience and knowledge, but you can make sure your letters present your experience and knowledge effectively.

- *Optimism.* Back to the optimism thing. While you sure don't want to sound like a Pollyanna, where everything is just rosy, you can choose to take the optimistic approach at every turn. Point out the downsides of your industry, but be sure to off-set them with the ways that you will work around those negatives. Use your business letters to show the side of you that can make things happen despite any odds against you.

The Business Plan

There are many purposes for sending letters regarding your business plan. They include:

- *Seeking information.* Many parts of a business plan require some research—e.g., industry information for marketing, location information, supplier information. While you can call people to get information, it's smart to send a letter to give people a heads-up that you are planning to call and the purpose for your call. The letter can provide some background information so the person can help you more effectively and efficiently.

- *Requesting help with financials.* You don't need to be a math wiz to do the financials for a business plan, but you should probably know a wiz. Request his or her help via a letter that provides background information about your industry and your plans and outlines what you might want from your wiz.

- *Soliciting background material.* A lot of people include background material in their business plans. Letters are often the best way to solicit photographs, industry intelligence, and information about what businesses in other markets are doing.

- *Handling legal and administrative matters.* For any new business, there will be licenses, permits, and other official business you will want to investigate and address in your business plan. Some things can be done quickly over the phone; for others you will need to write letters and send supporting materials.

Be Forthcoming

When approaching people to help with information for your business plan, be sure to tell them how you will be using the information and that others will be seeing the information. Your business plan should ultimately be in a formal presentation and you want people to know this is how you will be using the material you get from them.

Seeking Information for Business Plan 1

[Date]

[Name]
[Company]
[Address]
[City, State ZIP]

Dear [Mr./Ms. Last Name]:

I have long been a customer of your business and have long admired the way you operate. Your shop seems efficient and I always feel that I am the top priority when I bring my car there for repairs.

Currently I am putting together a business plan for a service business. My business is in [Industry], an industry quite different from yours, but I feel that there are similarities in the way customers are handled no matter what the industry. Would you mind if I called you to ask a few questions regarding your philosophy about customer service? I would also like to include a quote from you in my business plan.

I have enclosed a self-addressed, stamped postcard so you can reply by simply checking off in the appropriate places. Then I will call at whatever time you designate as best for you. I appreciate your time.

Sincerely,

[Your Name]
[Your Address, if not on letterhead]

Don't be shy about asking for information in all areas. This diligence can show a lender that you have thought about your business thoroughly.

Seeking Information for Business Plan 2

[Date]

[Name]
[Company]
[Address]
[City, State ZIP]

Dear [Mr./Ms. Last Name]:

I am in the process of putting together a business plan for my new business, [Company Name]. We will be mostly a retail business, with some mail order and Internet marketing.

Since many people are not familiar with your products, which of course will feature prominently in my business, I was hoping you could provide me with a few samples to photograph for my business plan.

I would especially like to be able to get shots of [Product Names]. Although you probably have photographs of your products that I might use, I would like to be able to showcase them using the unique furnishings and color scheme that will be part of the signature of my business.

Of course I will be happy to return your product samples in the same packaging and via the same shipping method as you use to send them. It will take me around 30 days to complete the photographing and make sure we have the shots I want. And I will be happy to send you a copy of my business plan once it is complete.

Sincerely,

[Your Name]
[Your Address, if not on letterhead]

Expect this kind of service from anyone who is critical to your business. Your suppliers are not just doing you a favor—your use of their products is good for their business too. Be specific about such matters as how long you will keep their products and how you will return them.

Seeking Information for Business Plan 3

[Date]

[Name]
[Company]
[Address]
[City, State ZIP]

Dear [Mr./Ms. Last Name],

Enclosed please find a brief survey that I hope you will take the time to fill out to help me to gather information for my business plan for the opening of my store, [Business Name].

You will also find a self-addressed, stamped envelope for the return of the survey. If you include your name and address, we will mail you coupons to use in our store once we are open. Please rest assured that we will not sell or rent or let any third party use our list of names and addresses. If you would like us to include your name and address in our store mailings of coupons and specials, please check the box on the survey. Otherwise, we will delete your address from our mailing list once we have sent the coupons.

Thanks very much for your time and we look forward to having you as a valued customer.

Sincerely,

[Your Name]
[Your Address, if not on letterhead]

Surveys are common ways of obtaining information. Make them as easy as possible for the recipient to do and return. And keep your cover letter short! People barely have time to complete surveys, let alone read lengthy accompanying material.

Seeking Information for Business Plan 4

[Date]

[Name]
[Company]
[Address]
[City, State ZIP]

Dear [Mr./Ms. Last Name]:

I am pleased that you are willing to serve as an advisor in the start-up phase of my business. I have enclosed my business plan as it currently stands. This is how it will look—cover stock, color, etc.—except that it will be much more polished, since I bound this by hand!

I would appreciate getting a resume, brief bio, and photo from you to include in the business plan. If I could get those within two weeks, I would greatly appreciate it.

Thank you.

Sincerely,

[Your Name]
[Your Address, if not on letterhead]

Never send materials to someone without at least a short cover letter.

Seeking Information for Business Plan 5

[Date]

[Name]
[Company]
[Address]
[City, State ZIP]

Dear [Mr./Ms. Last Name]:

I am in the process of putting together a business plan for [Company Name]. Once the business starts up, I will be needing regular printing services for flyers. I am hoping you would be interested in providing me some estimates for use in the financial section of my business plan.

I need at this point estimates for the following five items:

- Design and creation of a logo.

- Letterhead and envelopes. I would think 1000 of each to start would be fine.

- Business cards for three people. A couple boxes (500 total?) each should suffice.

- A four-color three-fold flyer with six photographs. 1000 copies will be sufficient. Perhaps you could quote on 2,500 and 5,000 copies as well, for my financial projections.

- Web site creation and hosting services.

I look forward to getting these figures from you as soon as possible.

Sincerely,

[Your Name]
[Your Address, if not on letterhead]

Seeking Information for Business Plan 6

[Date]

[Name]
[Company]
[Address]
[City, State ZIP]

Dear [Mr./Ms. Last Name]:

We met briefly last year in New Orleans at the [Trade Show Name]. The company I work for was exhibiting a few of your products. I was in the booth when you came by to make sure we had received everything we requested.

I will be attending the [Same Trade Show Name] in April in Orlando. I was hoping you might have time in your schedule to meet with me for an hour to help me as I pull together some information for a business plan for a start-up. I will be at the show all three days and my schedule is pretty open at the moment.

I hope you understand that I need to keep my plans confidential at the moment.

I look forward to hearing from you.

Sincerely,

[Your Name]
[Your Address, if not on letterhead]

Seeking Information for Business Plan 7

[Date]

[Name]
[Company]
[Address]
[City, State ZIP]

Dear [Mr./Ms. Last Name]:

As I put together a business plan for a company I am calling [Company Name], I am gathering business plans to use as models and compare with mine.

I admire how your company is run and how much you have grown in such a short time. Would it be possible to look at a copy of the business plan you used when you started your business three years ago? I would be happy to return it.

Sincerely,

[Your Name]
[Your Address, if not on letterhead]

Seeking Information for Business Plan 8

[Date]

[Name]
[Company]
[Address]
[City, State ZIP]

Dear [Mr./Ms. Last Name]:

I am putting together a business plan for a cleaning service. I am looking for several businesses that might allow me to "test clean" their stores in order to have a realistic sense of what is involved and to make sure my business plan is complete.

I will call you in a few days.

Sincerely,

[Your Name]
[Your Address, if not on letterhead]

You might have just called without first sending a letter, but you can print the letter and send a copy to a number of businesses, giving everyone a heads-up about your idea with a minimum of time and effort.

Seeking Information for Business Plan 9

[Date]

[Name]
[Company]
[Address]
[City, State ZIP]

Dear [Mr./Ms. Last Name]:

I am wrapping up the details of my business plan to purchase your company and I need some final pieces of information.

Could you please send me your resume? I think it is important to include it, since anyone reading my business plan will be interested to know that you will be staying on board for six months.

Also, I noticed the month-by-month sales figures for 2005 are missing. I know I have seen them, so I think that either your secretary or I simply misplaced them.

Thanks very much.

Sincerely,

[Your Name]
[Your Address, if not on letterhead]

Seeking Information for Business Plan 10

[Date]

[Name]
[Company]
[Address]
[City, State ZIP]

Dear [Mr./Ms. Last Name]:

Attached are the rough financials I put together to include in my business plan. I really appreciate that you have agreed to spend some time with them to help me make sure the numbers are realistic.

I look forward to getting your response sometime by the first of the month.

Sincerely,

[Your Name]
[Your Address, if not on letterhead]

Always solicit as many professionals as you can afford to help you make your business plan as complete and accurate as possible.

## Chapter 7

Letters Seeking Information for a Marketing Plan

The marketing plan is a key part of a business plan. This is the information that helps anyone who is instrumental in implementing the plan to be comfortable that you fully understand your business.

Your marketing plan will need to include many things that you may need to write letters to obtain:

- Information on the current state of the market, both locally and nationally
- Statistical information kept by state or federal government agencies
- General information from other organizations proving the value of your idea
- Quotes for possible use in ads, brochures, and other marketing materials

A Letter Is Best

In many cases, you might think it would be easier to pick up the phone or visit to ask for whatever you need, instead of sending letters. But a letter will do two important things:

- It will save you time and effort. Requesting information by letter frees you from running around from place to place, especially since for many things you will want to get three quotes.
- It will reduce errors. When you call and request such things as an ad kit, it is easy for the phone message to get lost or otherwise not reach the person responsible for sending out the materials. You're also relying on the person taking the phone request to write down the message accurately, to record exactly what you're request-

ing and your name and address and any other specifics. When you send a letter, the person who opens it can simply place it in the mailbox of the person responsible for sending out the materials.

Think Outside the Box

Think about unusual and interesting information that you could obtain to include in the marketing plan section of your business plan. Collect ideas of brochures and other print materials that catch your eye. Readers of your business plan will like to see that you have reached beyond the traditional and really looked at your business.

The best way to get ideas on what to request for your business plan is to look at sample business plans (preferably from successful start-ups!) and see what other people have included. Think about how such ideas apply to your industry or business idea.

Obtaining Information from Statewide Nonprofit

[Date]

[Name]
[Company]
[Address]
[City, State ZIP]

Dear [Mr./Ms. Last Name]:

I read in the September 2006 issue of the *Equine Report* about your independent study of the equine industry in the Pacific Northwest. I am putting together a business plan to open a tack shop and would like to obtain a copy of that report to include some of the statistics in my plan.

Enclosed is a check for $10, the cost indicated in the article. I look forward to receiving it.

When you send the report, could you also verify in writing that it is permissible for me to reproduce information from the report in my business plan?

Thank you.

Sincerely,

[Your Name]
[Your Address, if not on letterhead]

Never reprint anything without getting permission to do so. Permission in writing is always best.

Requesting Information from National Organization

[Date]
[Name]
[Company]
[Address]
[City, State ZIP]

Dear [Mr./Ms. Last Name]:

I am working on a business plan to open a mail order and Internet-based equine supplies business. I read in a recent issue of *U.S. Horse* that you sponsored an independent study of the horse industry in the U.S.

Please send me a copy of that study. I have enclosed a check for $25, the cost indicated in the article. I look forward to receiving it.

When you send the report, could you also verify that it is permissible for me to reprint from the report in my business plan?

Thanks very much.

Sincerely,

[Your Name]
[Your Address, if not on letterhead]

Letter to Another Company

[Date]

[Name]
[Company]
[Address]
[City, State ZIP]

Dear [Mr./Ms. Last Name]:

I am in the process of putting together a business plan to open a catering service in the Greater Lakes Region.

For the marketing plan component, I am hoping you might be able to provide me with some information regarding the lobster business in this area. I am interested in questions such as the following:

- Do people eat lobster in this area or do they usually eat it only when they visit the coast?

- Do you believe there is a market for a catering service that focuses on clambakes?

- Do you see lots of people ordering their own lobster to cook themselves?

- Has anyone ever expressed a desire for a clambake catering service in the area?

I would like to follow up with a phone call to get answers to these and related questions. Could you please e-mail me at [Address] with a convenient time to call?

Thanks very much.

Sincerely,

[Your Name]
[Your Address, if not on letterhead]

When you are planning to call people to ask questions, it is always courteous to inform them in advance with a letter describing the kinds of questions you intend to ask. And always ask them to let you know when it might be convenient to call.

Request for Bid on Logo Design

You could get a quote in person, of course, but it is always best to get at least three quotes for any work, which means a lot of running around. In this phase that probably is not cost- or time-effective. Remember: at this point you are only asking for a rough quote, not for the actual logo to be done. That will come later.

[Date]

[Name]
[Company]
[Address]
[City, State ZIP]

Dear [Mr./Ms. Last Name]:

I am putting together a marketing plan for my new business. I was hoping you could provide me a quote for designing a logo that I could include in the business plan.

My logo would be fairly simple, one color. I have enclosed a rough sketch of what I think it might look like.

Sincerely,

[Your Name]
[Your Address, if not on letterhead]

Request for Ad Rates

[Date]

[Name]
[Company]
[Address]
[City, State ZIP]

Dear [Mr./Ms. Last Name]:

I am opening a new business in [Town Name] and would like some quotes on advertising to include in my business plan.

Please let me know what it would cost to run a regular 1/3 page ad in your weekly newspaper.

Also, if you could send along your entire advertising kit, I would appreciate it.

Thank you very much.

Sincerely,

[Your Name]
[Your Address, if not on letterhead]

Any place selling ads will try to set you up with a rep. Don't get involved to that extent until you have actually opened your business. Again, you are just collecting information at this point.

Request for Print Materials from Another Business

[Date]

[Name]
[Company]
[Address]
[City, State ZIP]

Dear [Mr./Ms. Last Name]:

I was in your area recently and noticed one of your flyers in an office I was visiting. Your materials were very unique and I would love to do something similar for my business, [Company Name], for which I am currently writing the business plan.

Would it be possible for you to send me a full set of your marketing materials? I would be happy to pay a fee or at least the shipping costs.

Please let me know whether you are able to send me some materials. My e-mail address is [Address] and my phone number is [Number].

Thanks very much.

Sincerely,

[Your Name]
[Your Address, if not on letterhead]

Request for out-of-Print Book

[Date]

[Name]
[Company]
[Address]
[City, State ZIP]

Dear [Mr./Ms. Last Name]:

I am struggling to write the marketing plan section of my business plan. I have learned that your company published a book on this very topic called [Title] by [Author] in [Year]. I know that it is out of print and I have not been able to find a copy anywhere.

Do you have a copy of this book in your inventory that I could purchase? If you could e-mail me at [Address] or call me at [Number], I would very much appreciate it.

Sincerely,

[Your Name]
[Your Address, if not on letterhead]

Sometimes you need to go right to the source. Again, this is a request that it is better to make in a letter: the person receiving it can simply pass the letter to someone who could look for the book.

Request for Materials from Chamber of Commerce

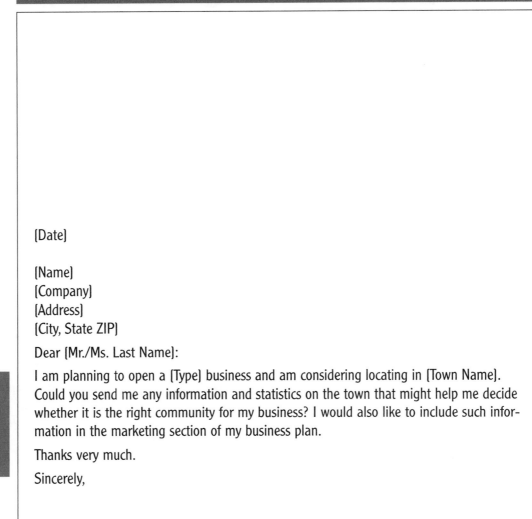

[Date]

[Name]
[Company]
[Address]
[City, State ZIP]

Dear [Mr./Ms. Last Name]:

I am planning to open a [Type] business and am considering locating in [Town Name]. Could you send me any information and statistics on the town that might help me decide whether it is the right community for my business? I would also like to include such information in the marketing section of my business plan.

Thanks very much.

Sincerely,

[Your Name]
[Your Address, if not on letterhead]

A chamber of commerce can be a very good source of statistical information about an area.

Requesting Review of Marketing Plan

[Date]

[Name]
[Company]
[Address]
[City, State ZIP]

Dear [Mr./Ms. Last Name]:

Thank you so much for agreeing to review the marketing section of my business plan. I have always trusted your judgment and admired your marketing sense and I know you will be a keen and critical eye.

Please keep in mind that this is an early draft. You can suggest anything you think would help; I have time to make any changes you might suggest. And if you know of any sources for hard numbers that I could include in my plan, I would appreciate any suggestions.

I have enclosed a self-addressed, stamped envelope so you can return this draft with your comments.

Thanks for your time and attention.

Sincerely,

[Your Name]
[Your Address, if not on letterhead]

If you expect someone to return something to you, always, always include a self-addressed, stamped envelope.

Seeking Meeting

Again, think outside the box about which people you might talk with about the market for your business. Competitors obviously don't want to chat with you, but many types of businesses are targeting the same customers with their different products and services.

[Date]

[Name]
[Company]
[Address]
[City, State ZIP]

Dear [Mr./Ms. Last Name]:

I am writing a business plan to open a [Business Type]. Although your business is in a completely separate industry and I would not be competing with you in any way, I feel my target market would be the same kind of customers.

Would you be able to spare an hour of your time to sit and talk with me so I might get a better feel for the buying attitudes of this customer base? I want to be able to include this information in the marketing section of my business plan.

I will call you within a few days after you receive this letter to see if we can set up a time to meet.

Thank you very much.

Sincerely,

[Your Name]
[Your Address, if not on letterhead]

## Chapter 8

Letters Seeking Financing

Letters seeking financing for your business do not need to be lengthy or complicated, as they will usually be accompanied by your business plan, which should speak for itself. However, you want to emphasize the positive information that the reader will find in your business plan, such as the following:

- *The financial statements.* This is where almost any potential lender is going first, especially financial people like bankers and venture capitalists. For them, the numbers say it all.

- *Your credentials.* Your ability to start up and manage a business is key to its success, so use your cover letter to direct potential lenders to this area of your business plan.

- *The market.* How well your business does depends ultimately on the numbers of customers out there who might use your product or service. Point out the key factors in the marketing section of your business plan that prove that there are enough potential customers for profitability.

- *Potential for growth.* Although your start-up business plan won't include much material on the future of your business, potential financial partners and investors will want to at least see some thought about how your business might be able to grow as it matures.

To Whom You Might Send Letters

You may be seeking financing from a few types of people—family members, friends, business acquaintances—and institutions. Your letters will need to vary in tone and content according to the recipients. Your Aunt Claire isn't going to be interested in the same information as First National Bank and she probably won't respond well if your letter addresses her in the same tone as it addresses the banker.

Keep your letter short and polite. Do not grumble about the difficulties, even to friends and family. Be businesslike and sound like you really know what you are talking about. And, as always, proofread your letters!

Letter to Bank 1

[Date]

[Name]
[Company]
[Address]
[City, State ZIP]

Dear [Mr./Ms. Last Name]:

I am a long-time customer of [Bank Name] and am turning to you first as I seek financing for my start-up business, [Company Name].

Enclosed you will find my business plan. Let me point out some things that would be of particular interest to you in reviewing this plan.

Market: You will note that the potential market for my product is huge. Not only is the number of pets in the U.S. at an all-time high, but their owners are spending record amounts of money on caring for them.

Financials: You will also note that I do not need much start-up capital. I should be able to balance the production of my product quite nicely with sales in order to keep inventory just a notch above "just-in-time" levels.

I should point out too that I am very familiar with the pet industry. I have been working at All-Pet for seven years, which is how I became aware of this gap in the market and the opportunity.

Please let me know if you need anything else to help you decide to lend me the start-up capital and six months' operating expenses I am requesting.

I look forward to hearing from you.

Sincerely,

[Your Name]
[Your Address, if not on letterhead]

Keep everything in your letter positive. Don't say such things as "I know this is a tough time in the market, but …."

Letter to Bank 2

[Date]

[Name]
[Company]
[Address]
[City, State ZIP]

Dear [Mr./Ms. Last Name]:

I am looking forward to speaking with your regarding my request for a loan for my new business, [Business Name].

Enclosed you will find the information you requested to further support the point I am making in my business plan about the ultimate potential of such a retail store and just exactly how the franchise works.

Please let me know if you need anything else.

Sincerely,

[Your Name]
[Your Address, if not on letterhead]

You will probably hand this information to a receptionist or an assistant to give to the loan officer with whom you are working, but a cover letter should still accompany it.

Letter to Private Investor 1

[Date]

[Name]
[Company]
[Address]
[City, State ZIP]

Dear [Mr./Ms. Last Name]:

Enclosed you will find the full business plan for my start-up service company, [Company Name]. With people leading busier and busier lives, the service sector in the U.S. has exploded. I have a unique and carefully planned approach to enter that market.

My bank, [Bank Name], is willing to lend me the start-up capital I need if I can find funding for the operating capital. This funding cannot require payments to begin until I have paid off the bank's loan, which will be in five years.

I am hoping you will see that this is a valuable business in which to invest. In my 12 years in the same industry, I have proven that I am not afraid of hard work; I know I will work at least as hard for my own business as I have for others.

Please let me know if you have any questions.

Sincerely,

[Your Name]
[Your Address, if not on letterhead]

Be upfront in your letter about any side agreements or details, like in this instance the need to pay off the bank loan first. Although it may seem like you should first get the potential investor revved up about your business before revealing such facts, you are better just bringing them up from the beginning, since at this stage of your business you definitely want to avoid wasting any time.

Letter to Private Investor 2

[Date]

[Name]
[Company]
[Address]
[City, State ZIP]

Dear [Mr./Ms. Last Name]:

I got your name from [Name], who said you were very helpful when she was starting up her business, [Company Name]. I think you will see similar potential in my business as you did in hers.

I have enclosed my complete business plan for your review. I am asking for [Amount] to cover start-up costs and six months of operating expenses. I believe this is a comfortable amount to ensure that I can start off right, yet not so high that it represents a considerable risk.

I am happy to discuss whatever repayment schedule you would require. Please let me know if you need any further information.

I look forward to talking with you.

Sincerely,

[Your Name]
[Your Address, if not on letterhead]

By talking about a repayment schedule and low risk, this letter ever so subtly implies that the potential investor is already considering agreeing to the loan. As with product advertising, you have to make that person feel what it would be like having lent you the money, without being pushy and presumptuous.

Letter to Venture Capitalist 1

[Date]

[Name]
[Company]
[Address]
[City, State ZIP]
Dear [Mr./Ms. Last Name]:

My business plan for a manufacturing plant for [Industry] is enclosed. I appreciate your interest in my project. Here are some things I would like to point out before we meet next Friday:

- The building is available for long-term lease beginning in September of next year.

- I am paying upfront to have prototypes and molds made. The prototypes are almost done; I hope to be able to bring one with me on Friday.

- There are places where I could trim the figures, but this business plan and financial represent what I believe is the best-case scenario for success.

I look forward to meeting you.

Sincerely,

[Your Name]
[Your Address, if not on letterhead]

Precede any financing meetings with a business plan accompanied by a cover letter.

Letter to Venture Capitalist 2

Venture capitalists are shrewd businesspeople. You will need all that you've got to make them comfortable with your idea.

[Date]

[Name]
[Company]
[Address]
[City, State ZIP]

Dear [Mr./Ms. Last Name]:

The vending machine business is mature, but I believe I have a different angle on it that could be very profitable. I am enclosing my business plan, a copy for you and each of your colleagues. I hope you find it intriguing enough to meet with me in the near future.

Use of vending in this manner has been tried but without success. After much research and experimenting, I have found the key to making it work. I look forward to talking with you about how you can be part of this exciting venture.

Sincerely,

[Your Name]
[Your Address, if not on letterhead]

Letter to Family Member 1

[Date]

[Name]
[Company]
[Address]
[City, State ZIP]

Dear [Uncle/Aunt/Name]:

How are Sue and Al? I hope Sue and her family are surviving the Texas heat wave! We had so much fun when we visited them this spring. And I appreciate her mentioning my business to you and your willingness to consider contributing financially.

The business plan is enclosed. I have a commitment for the start-up costs, but I really need to gather six months' worth of operating capital before I quit my job and dive in. It is very exciting and I am eager to get going now that I am so close!

I am looking for a total of $50,000. I do not expect to get that from one source; in fact, I am thinking about getting ten contributors at $5,000 each. My brother is investing $10,000, so that means I only need to find eight more. I have three investors who are forgoing interest in exchange for use of the facility when it is complete. Of course, an arrangement like that wouldn't help you, so I would expect to pay you interest at 5%, which is higher than CDs and other low-risk investments at this moment.

Let me know what you think of my business plan and if you think you might want to invest. And please, be sure you [and Name] visit the next time you are out this way.

Sincerely,

[Your Name]
[Your Address, if not on letterhead]

Sometimes family members are more likely to decide to invest if they know that other family members and/or friends have invested.

Letter to Family Member 2

If you borrow from a family member, always point out that you plan to have a legal agreement drafted that makes it perfectly clear what is expected—and then do what you agree to do! That is the best way to avoid feuding with family members over a loan.

[Date]

[Name]
[Company]
[Address]
[City, State ZIP]

Dear [Uncle/Aunt/Name]:

I enjoyed talking with you last night and I am thrilled that you are interested in reviewing my business plan and potentially investing in my business. It is one of those odd situations: typical investors don't want to lend me money because I am not asking for enough!

I guess that means I could be starting bigger, but I feel like I am being realistic. My idea is great and I know it will succeed, but I would like to grow my business modestly.

My business plan says it all, with all of the numbers, but of course if you have any questions, please call! I would intend to have a lawyer draft a formal agreement between us and I would pay interest monthly, quarterly, annually, or however you and I think works best.

Again, thanks, [Uncle/Aunt/Name], for considering this opportunity!

Sincerely,

[Your Name]
[Your Address, if not on letterhead]

Letter to Friend 1

[Date]

[Name]
[Company]
[Address]
[City, State ZIP]

Dear [Name]:

Thank you so much for expressing interest in investing in my business. I am enclosing two copies of my business plan—one for you and one to bring to your investment club for the members to review. I appreciate that thought—it is an excellent idea! If you and your colleagues have any interest in a presentation, I am happy to do that. Of course, I am available to answer any questions as well.

Sincerely,

[Your Name]
[Your Address, if not on letterhead]

Letter to Friend 2

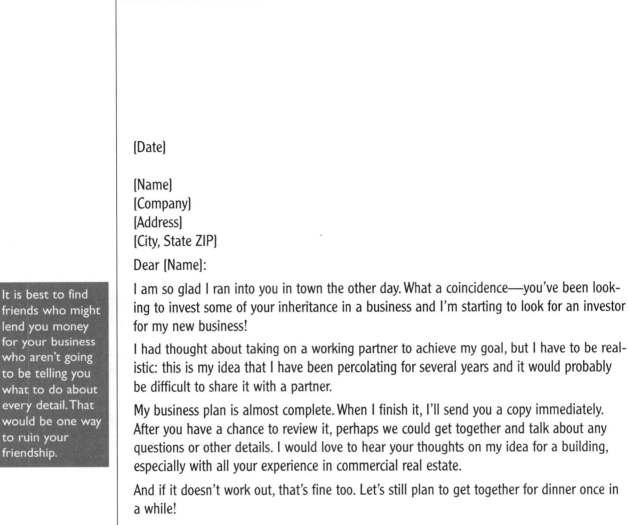

[Date]

[Name]
[Company]
[Address]
[City, State ZIP]

Dear [Name]:

I am so glad I ran into you in town the other day. What a coincidence—you've been looking to invest some of your inheritance in a business and I'm starting to look for an investor for my new business!

I had thought about taking on a working partner to achieve my goal, but I have to be realistic: this is my idea that I have been percolating for several years and it would probably be difficult to share it with a partner.

My business plan is almost complete. When I finish it, I'll send you a copy immediately. After you have a chance to review it, perhaps we could get together and talk about any questions or other details. I would love to hear your thoughts on my idea for a building, especially with all your experience in commercial real estate.

And if it doesn't work out, that's fine too. Let's still plan to get together for dinner once in a while!

Sincerely,

[Your Name]
[Your Address, if not on letterhead]

It is best to find friends who might lend you money for your business who aren't going to be telling you what to do about every detail. That would be one way to ruin your friendship.

Letters for Operation

## Chapter 9

Sales Letters

Sales letters are probably among the most common business letters you will write. And perhaps the most important, since without sales you have no business! Here are some of the types of sales letters you will be writing:

- *Prospecting letters.* You needn't be shy about prospecting if you target people who are truly potential customers for your products or services.

- *Cover letters* to accompany catalogs, fliers, information sheets, and special offers. This is a great way to increase sales by pointing out items of special interest.

- *Proposal letters* for taking on new products, services, etc.

- *Introductory letters* to arrange sales calls. The appointments are usually made by phone, but an introductory letter can help get your foot in the door.

- *Follow-up letters.* These are a very good way to outline in writing what you and the recipient have discussed in a meeting or phone call and what you two (and maybe others) have decided so all parties are on the same page.

- *Referral letters.*

- *Announcement letters.* Write a letter to announce anything important, especially that recipients might want to have in writing, such as changes in discount schedules or credit terms.

- *Sales management letters.*

- *Sales appreciation letters.* Letters of appreciation are always a simple way to acknowledge a customer's business.

There are some important factors to consider when writing sales correspondence.

- Check and recheck your letter for accuracy. The difference between "can" or "can't" is huge when it comes to outlining credit terms, discounts, etc.

- Identify your potential customer's need and keep that in the forefront. Successful sales letters are not about what you have to sell; they are about what the potential customer needs and how you can satisfy that need.

- Never sign off a sales letter without making it totally clear what the recipient should do. Do not expect him or her to figure these things out. You are asking for the sale, so it's in your best interests to make purchasing as easy as possible.

- Keep your tone conversational but avoid being flip. For most people, solving their needs and parting with money are serious business.

With that in mind, let's get to some sample letters.

Prospecting 1

[Date]

[Name]
[Company]
[Address]
[City, State ZIP]

Dear [Mr./Ms. Last Name]:

I enjoyed our conversation on the flight from Dallas to Boston last week. Thanks so much for the tip on digital cameras. I bought one just like yours this weekend and I have already taken tons of great pictures!

You mentioned you work with party planners and I wanted to make sure you know about my business selling paper goods. I've enclosed a flier of what [Company Name] offers. I hope you will consider recommending us to your contacts. We sell nationwide and we take great pride in offering unique, high-quality products.

Good luck with your upcoming retreat.

Sincerely,

[Your Name]
[Your Address, if not on letterhead]

Meeting prospective clients while traveling is common. Always ask people for a business card and always follow up. Remind them in the beginning of the letter how you met.

Prospecting 2

[Date]

[Name]
[Company]
[Address]
[City, State ZIP]

Dear [Mr./Ms. Last Name]:

My sign company, [Company Name], is creating a sign for a business near yours, [Company Name].

On Monday afternoon, [Date], I am going to walk around the neighborhood, introduce myself, and talk with neighboring businesses about how my sign company can help you bring attention to your business.

I have enclosed our brochure that shows some examples of our work, of which we are extremely proud. Our designer would be happy to create some ideas for you to look at.

I hope you will be around on Monday so you and I can meet.

Sincerely,

[Your Name]
[Your Address, if not on letterhead]

Use sales to create sales. A letter of introduction to businesses located near a client is a great opportunity to generate sales leads.

Prospecting 3

[Date]

[Name]
[Company]
[Address]
[City, State ZIP]

Dear [Mr./Ms. Last Name]:

I am pleased to announce that your neighbors, [Names], have sold their home at 555 Main Street. They listed their home with our real estate firm, [Company Name], just two and a half months ago.

If you have been thinking about selling your home, now is a great time. The real estate market in your area is booming as buyers realize the value of moving away from the busy seacoast area and getting more home for their dollar.

I would love to help you through the home sale process. The first step is the appraisal process. And I can help give you tips on what you need to do to get your home ready to show and sell. Then I hope you think of me when you are ready to sell—I can help you find your next home too!

I look forward to working with you.

Sincerely,

[Your Name]
[Your Business and Address, if not on letterhead]

Your sales prospecting letters should place the recipient right in the sale. In this case, help the recipient visualize selling his or her home and buying another. And make the point that you can help make something that seems like a daunting task become relatively easy.

Cover Letter with Catalog 1

So many catalogs get delivered to our mailboxes. Use a cover letter to tell recipients how your catalog stands out from the crowd and why they should open it up.

[Date]

[Name]
[Company]
[Address]
[City, State ZIP]

Dear [Mr./Ms. Last Name]:

Most fall clothing catalogs have left swimsuits far behind. But we know you are planning your winter vacation to a warm spot, so we have kept two full pages of our most popular and flattering swimsuits and sandals.

But we didn't forget fall either! Just because the leaves are falling, there is no need to be dreary! Fabulous fall colors are used in unique ways in everything from sweaters and vests to accessories like belts and scarves.

And if you act fast, you can take advantage of our limited time offer of free shipping on all orders over $50.

As always, thanks for your business.

Sincerely,

[Your Name]
[Your Address, if not on letterhead]

Cover Letter for Catalog 2

[Date]

[Name]
[Company]
[Address]
[City, State ZIP]

Dear [Mr./Ms. Last Name]:

[Company Name] has been providing you with access to the finest fishing gear in the world for over 50 years. Now, we are proud to have teamed up with [Company 2 Name] to offer you the finest outdoor clothing. [Company 2 Name] has been in the business of making high-quality outerwear for over 50 years as well. That's 100 years of experience brought right to your door in this catalog!

To help celebrate this joint venture, we are offering 10% off your first order. With fishing season just around the corner, we've made your shopping as easy as sitting in the recliner with a cup of coffee. You can order either over the phone or online at our secure Web site, [URL].

Sincerely,

[Your Name]
[Your Address, if not on letterhead]

A new venture is always reason to announce your catalog with a cover letter. Remember to include your Web site URL in all your correspondence.

Special Offer 1

A special offer to entice new customers is a good reason to spend any extra it might cost to include a letter with a catalog.

[Date]

[Name]
[Company]
[Address]
[City, State ZIP]

Dear [Mr./Ms. Last Name]:

Just think—never again do you have to open the coffee can and find just one scoop left. We are so sure that once you try our mail order coffee service you will wonder how you ever lived without it—so sure that we are offering a free coffeemaker with your initial subscription.

Our service is customized to meet your coffee-drinking preferences. You can increase or decrease your order at any time by simply visiting our Web site, [URL],) and adjusting your subscription. The enclosed catalog shows the many flavors in both caffeinated and decaffeinated you can choose. And all of our coffee is 100% organically grown, so you the taste you get is pure coffee.

Act now and get your free coffeemaker. We look forward to you joining the [Company Name] family of discriminating coffee drinkers.

Sincerely,

[Your Name]
[Your Address, if not on letterhead]

Special Offer 2

[Date]

[Name]
[Company]
[Address]
[City, State ZIP]

Dear [Mr./Ms. Last Name]:

We appreciate your loyalty over the past five years and have been honored to serve you with the highest-quality merchandise and great customer service for which [Company Name] has become known.

As a token of our appreciation, we would like to make you a special offer: Bring us three new customers and we will give you a 10% discount off all of your purchases from [Company Name] for the next year!

Spread the word and you save! It's as easy as that. New customers can sign on via our Web site at [URL]. Be sure they indicate in the space provided that you referred them to us. And just for signing on, they get a 10% discount off their first order.

It's a win-win-win for all!

Sincerely,

[Your Name]
[Your Address, if not on letterhead]

Customers love being acknowledged for their loyalty. Loyalty programs (e.g., buy 10 sandwiches, get one free) have long been considered to pay all off well. And why not gain a few customers in the process?

Price Increase

Not only is change difficult for people, but change in pricing is especially unwelcome. Don't hide price increases and certainly don't spring them on your customers. A letter being upfront about it, giving your customers as much notice as possible and reminding them of the benefits of doing business with you, can go a long way toward retaining customers.

[Date]

[Name]
[Company]
[Address]
[City, State ZIP]

Dear [Mr./Ms. Last Name]:

We have been proud to maintain our fees for three years now, but with the significant increase in fuel prices we have had to look carefully at our pricing structure. I am sorry to report that we are increasing our prices; however, I am pleased to report that we did not have to increase them as much as I had feared.

As a loyal customer, I wanted to forewarn you of this price increase immediately so that you can adjust your budgeting and financial projections accordingly.

Our new pricing structure is attached and it goes into effect beginning [Date]. Please restock accordingly. If there is anything I can do to ease the burden of this new pricing structure, please feel free to call and we can discuss possibilities.

Please be assured that we are as committed as ever to giving you the best possible service to help your business be successful. Our quality products with timely, efficient on-time delivery will continue to help your business thrive.

Sincerely,

[Your Name]
[Your Address, if not on letterhead]

New Product Announcement

[Date]

[Name]
[Company]
[Address]
[City, State ZIP]

Dear [Mr./Ms. Last Name]:

You are one of the thousands of customers who have enjoyed our water cooler, providing you and your employees with clean drinking water. We are pleased to announce a new product that will put an end to the need to find the strongest employee to change the water bottle or to get the mop handy to clean up the inevitable spill.

We have redesigned our popular hot/cold water system so that the water bottle now goes on the bottom of the cooler. Earlier designs used gravity feed to bring the water to the spigot. Since the hot water delivery requires electricity anyway, we added a pump to bring the water up the cooler, making it possible to keep the jug at the bottom. Now you simply roll the jug across the floor, insert the tubing into the jug, and stand the jug in place in the cabinet.

The WaterSystem 1000 is ready for you now. We are offering an introductory 10% discount off the purchase price, along with six free five-gallon jugs of water.

So put the mop back into the closet and order your WaterSystem 1000 today!

Sincerely,

[Your Name]
[Your Address, if not on letterhead]

Be sure to point out the benefits of any new product.

New Ownership

[Date]

[Name]
[Company]
[Address]
[City, State ZIP]

Dear [Mr./Ms. Last Name]:

I would like to congratulate you on your purchase of [Recipient's Company Name]. [Name of Former Owner] and I have done business for over 20 years. Our company, [Company Name], has been providing [Recipient's Company Name] products for all their paper needs for all of that time.

[Recipient's Company Name] is an important customer and I want to be sure we help in any way we can to make sure the transition of ownership goes smoothly. To that end, I will call you next week to set up an appointment to meet.

I look forward to many more years of a productive relationship between [Recipient's Company Name] and [Company Name].

Sincerely,

[Your Name]
[Your Address, if not on letterhead]

When a client business changes hands, jump right on the opportunity to meet the new owner face to face and discuss the productive relationship the businesses have had over the years and how your company has helped the business.

Maintenance Complaint

[Date]

[Name]
[Company]
[Address]
[City, State ZIP]

Dear [Mr./Ms. Last Name]:

Thank you for your time in discussing your concern regarding the recent maintenance of our photocopiers in your office. As I said on the phone, your concerns are important to us and critical for us to maintain the high level of service that we constantly strive to achieve.

I have spoken with the service contractor. He has assured me that the type of incident that occurred between your employee and the service repair person will not happen again.

We also agreed that it is time for us to create a more useful manual for our machines. This topic has come up in the past and we have been negligent in not doing this sooner.

We have formed a team to work on this task. A team member will be calling you in the near future to get feedback to help us make this manual as useful as possible. In the meantime, we have arranged for your company to get a free seminar outlining the many uses of our machines that are not as well known. And we are sending a case of paper with our compliments.

I look forward to continuing our good relationship. If you experience any further problems or have any questions, please feel free to call.

Sincerely,

[Your Name]
[Your Address, if not on letterhead]

Be careful not to blame the company, even if your service contractor said the company employees were using the photocopiers to blend coffee. And always offer to be available for questions and concerns.

Sales Lapse

[Date]

[Name]
[Company]
[Address]
[City, State ZIP]

Dear [Mr./Ms. Last Name]:

We have noticed that lately you have been buying from us much less frequently and we are wondering if there is a problem. If you are dissatisfied with our products or service, please call and discuss the problem. I am certain we can fix it.

To give you an incentive to order, I have enclosed a discount coupon good on your next order. And if you place a standing order for the next year, we will extend that discount to the entire year's purchases.

We look forward to doing business with you regularly again.

Sincerely,

[Your Name]
[Your Address, if not on letterhead]

Lapsed customers sometimes just need a little reminder, a little special attention. Use coupons to get them ordering and try to find out the reason for the lapse.

Sales Call Confirmation

[Date]

[Name]
[Company]
[Address]
[City, State ZIP]

Dear [Mr./Ms. Last Name]:

Congratulations on opening your new surveying business. We are pleased that you have chosen [Company Name] to provide you with the quality instruments you need as professionals.

I am writing to confirm our appointment on [Date] at [Time]. I've enclosed several copies of our product catalog for you and your team to review prior to our meeting. This will give you a chance to make note of any questions you or your team members may have. I will bring many of our products so I can demonstrate the superior quality and usability of our surveying tools. [Company Name] is proud to offer a complete line of almost everything you will need to get your company up and running.

I look forward to meeting you on [Date]. If you have any questions in the meantime, please do not hesitate to call me.

Sincerely,

[Your Name]
[Your Address, if not on letterhead]

Sales appointment confirmation letters should outline your objectives for the meeting, tell how the recipient should prepare for the meeting, and of course confirm the date and time you've agreed to meet.

Sales Call Letter

[Date]

[Name]
[Company]
[Address]
[City, State ZIP]

Dear [Mr./Ms. Last Name]:

It seems impossible, but six months has passed since you began using our payroll service. We at [Company Name] appreciate your business. Although I trust that things are going smoothly for you, I'd like to meet with you to review the first six months of our relationship. Please let me know when it would be convenient for you.

I will want to review the services you have been using over the past six months and consider whether there are any additional services that would benefit you or any services you don't use that we should remove from your menu. It would be helpful to our discussion if you could consult with your accounting team and plan to have one or two key people attend our meeting.

In the meantime, don't hesitate to call if anything comes up that needs more immediate attention.

Sincerely,

[Your Name]
[Your Address, if not on letterhead]

Don't hesitate to suggest inviting other personnel who may be able to contribute to your meeting in beneficial ways, paving the way to signing on additional services.

Sales Letter

[Date]

[Name]
[Company]
[Address]
[City, State ZIP]
Dear [Mr./Ms. Last Name]:
This letter is to confirm that your parents are booked for a two-week stay in our cottages on Lake Swan from Saturday July 12th to Saturday July 26th. They are welcome to arrive any time after 3 pm on the 12th and we expect them to leave by 10 am on the 26th. You also want us to provide catering for two events:

- a welcoming breakfast on Sunday July 13th for eight people
- a 50th anniversary party on Saturday afternoon July 19th for 40 people

We will be calling you June 20th at 3 pm to discuss the details of these two events. Some things you might want to be thinking about in the meantime are:

- Do you want us to decorate for these events?

- Do your parents or their guests have any dietary considerations?

- Do you want the anniversary party to be a sit-down dinner or a stand-and-mingle affair with a buffet?

- Are these surprise events?

- Do you want any activities, such as a cruise around the lake or rental paddle boats available?

- Will there be children? If so, how would you like to accommodate them? Do you need a child care provider?

There are a lot of considerations, but I can walk you through them when we talk. We have been providing the most memorable events on Lake Swan for 25 years and we have endless ideas and contacts to make your parents' stay with us most enjoyable.

Sincerely,

[Your Name]
[Your Address, if not on letterhead]

> Use your confirmation letter to begin to upsell other products or services you provide.

Sales Follow-up Letter 1

[Date]

[Name]
[Company]
[Address]
[City, State ZIP]

Dear [Mr./Ms. Last Name]:

We appreciate your considering [Company Name] to bid on your septic system upgrade. We commend you on your decision to create an environmentally sensitive septic system for the safety of your family and your neighbors as well as for maintaining the value of your home.

Based on our site visit last week, we present the attached estimate of our services. At the bottom of the estimate you will find a list of things that can reduce the cost, such as seeding the site yourself.

Also please note that, as we discussed, the quote is based on a worst-case scenario, considering the small size of the area in which we will be working. There is a very good chance that we can work around at least some of these issues and the cost will come down in the long run.

This quote is good for 30 days. We will contact you within that time to see if you have made a decision. We are confident that you will be pleased with our work. I am happy to provide names and numbers of recent clients if you would like to get references for our work.

Sincerely,

[Your Name]
[Your Address, if not on letterhead]

Few clients contact references for things like home renovations, but by offering them you can reassure potential customers and encourage trust.

Sales Follow-up Letter 2

[Date]

[Name]
[Company]
[Address]
[City, State ZIP]

Dear [Mr./Ms. Last Name]:

It has been a month since we installed your color copier/fax/printer and I am following up to be sure it is meeting your needs.

I have enclosed a customer satisfaction card, so you can help us serve you better. We hope you will take a few minutes to fill it out and return it. It is already stamped and addressed so you can simply slip it into the mail.

Thanks for your business. If there is anything further I can do for you, please don't hesitate to call.

Sincerely,

[Your Name]
[Your Address, if not on letterhead]

Following up on a sale is a great time to get feedback. Don't miss out on this opportunity.

Sales Follow-up Letter 3

[Date]

[Name]
[Company]
[Address]
[City, State ZIP]

Dear [Mr./Ms. Last Name]:

We hope you are enjoying your [Company Name] hot tub we installed at your cabin last month.

In appreciation for your purchase, we are enclosing a coupon worth $50 for cleaning supplies. Taking appropriate care of your hot tub is essential to keeping it operating smoothly so you continue to enjoy it for many years to come.

I've also enclosed a few postcards for you to give your friends. If they return them to us for further information about our hot tubs, we will send you more coupons for valuable products—and include your name in a drawing for a weekend for two at the [Name] resort in [City], [State]! All that just for telling your friends how they can relax in a hot tub at the end of a long work day like you do!

Sincerely,

[Your Name]
[Your Address, if not on letterhead]

Always find ways to give your satisfied customers incentives to tell their friends—your potential customers—about your great products.

Sales Follow-up Letter 4

[Date]

[Name]
[Company]
[Address]
[City, State ZIP]

Dear [Mr./Ms. Last Name]:

You purchased our workbook, [Title], at the [Seminar Name] in [Month]. I hope it has been providing you with valuable instruction for improving your skills.

I thought you would like to know about a new book hot off the press—[Title]. This is a natural follow-on for the book you purchased in February.

If you order now with the enclosed coupon, you will get the same discount as we give for purchases made at our seminars. But hurry—this offer only lasts until [Date].

You also will want to look at the enclosed list of upcoming seminars. The [Upcoming Seminar Name] is a perfect next step after the [Seminar Name] you attended in [Month]. And if you sign up now, we are offering a 10% discount on the seminar.

Join us!

Sincerely,

[Your Name]
[Your Address, if not on letterhead]

Use discounts with time limits to get people to act now and not just file your letter and fliers away in a "maybe" pile to which they will likely never return.

New Sales Representative

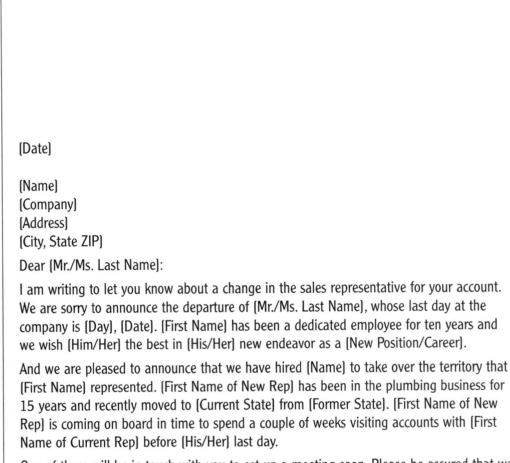

[Date]

[Name]
[Company]
[Address]
[City, State ZIP]

Dear [Mr./Ms. Last Name]:

I am writing to let you know about a change in the sales representative for your account. We are sorry to announce the departure of [Mr./Ms. Last Name], whose last day at the company is [Day], [Date]. [First Name] has been a dedicated employee for ten years and we wish [Him/Her] the best in [His/Her] new endeavor as a [New Position/Career].

And we are pleased to announce that we have hired [Name] to take over the territory that [First Name] represented. [First Name of New Rep] has been in the plumbing business for 15 years and recently moved to [Current State] from [Former State]. [First Name of New Rep] is coming on board in time to spend a couple of weeks visiting accounts with [First Name of Current Rep] before [His/Her] last day.

One of them will be in touch with you to set up a meeting soon. Please be assured that we expect a smooth transition. We value your business. If you have any questions now or in the future, I welcome you to contact me directly.

Sincerely,

[Your Name]
[Your Address, if not on letterhead]

Change is hard for lots of people. Anything you can do to offset any negative feelings and be sure your clients don't jump ship during a time of change is time well spent.

## Chapter 10

Customer Service Letters

Letters to your current customers are some of the most important letters you will write. The old saying that the satisfied customer will tell one or two other people but the dissatisfied customer will tell a dozen or more people about their bad experience is oh so true. Well-crafted and timely letters will help your customers think positively about your business. Some of the most egregious mistakes can be smoothed over with a good letter from the appropriate person in the company. Letters to your customers are simply a great way to build a great relationship with the people who are critical to your business.

Customer service letters, particularly those responding to complaints, can be a little longer than unsolicited sales letters. But don't go on forever. If the key information in your response to a customer's complaint is buried in several paragraphs, your customer won't get to it before he or she tosses the letter away.

There are at least four types of customer service letter:

- *Confirmation letters* confirm information that you and the customer have exchanged, such as the delivery date and time of a product or service, the date of a meeting, or a customer's order.

- *Thank-you letters* never go out of fashion—send them and send them often. Thank customers for being loyal, for trying your business for the first time, for recommending you to their friends and family, and for other things they do for your company.

- *Follow-up letters* are a great way to prove to customers that you do what you say you will. If you promise to get them some information or to send a brochure or to give them a quote, do it. And follow up with a letter. You will follow up with a phone call, too, but letters are a great way to leave a paper trail of your contacts and to give people time to think about things before talking on the phone.

- *Credit and collection letters* are where you need to be direct and firm. This is no place to mince words (unless you are dealing internationally, which is addressed in Chapter 18). First and foremost, ask for payment! Then be sure to clearly spell out the essential details: how much the customer owes, when it was due, and what you are going to do next if the customer does not pay immediately.

Confirmation Letter 1

[Date]

[Name]
[Company]
[Address]
[City, State ZIP]

Dear [Mr./Ms. Last Name]:

Thanks so much for your order. Here are the details as we discussed them when I was in your shop on Thursday:

- 500 units of the [Product], item [Number], shipping costs paid by us

- delivery the week of [Date]

- you are free to return unused [Products] by [Date], shipping costs paid by you

- invoice to be paid within 30 days of returned merchandise or by [Date], whichever comes first

Please call me if any of these details are incorrect.

I appreciate your order.

Sincerely,

[Your Name]
[Your Address, if not on letterhead]

Using a follow-up letter to confirm an order and itemize the details of delivery and payment is a great way to avoid any misinterpretations and to let your customer know he or she is important to you.

Confirmation Letter 2

Use a brief follow-up letter to thank clients for their business, to reiterate main details, and to remind them of any follow-up they were going to do.

[Date]

[Name]
[Company]
[Address]
[City, State ZIP]

Dear [Mr./Ms. Last Name]:

I enjoyed meeting with you both on Saturday. Your renovation project is exciting and I am looking forward to beginning the design!

Here are the things you said were most important for your mudroom project:

- use the existing space as efficiently as possible
- open up a little to let more light into the room
- create a somewhat sophisticated country look
- make the flooring be pet-proof
- provide cabinet and storage space and places for coats and boots

I will get back to you with more details and an estimate. In the meantime, feel free to contact me and modify this list if you think of anything else or see any ideas that appeal to you. And please, if you find them, send me those pages out of the magazine you mentioned that had the mudroom you liked and thought was pretty close to what you want.

Sincerely,

[Your Name]
[Your Address, if not on letterhead]

Confirmation Letter 3

[Date]

[Name]
[Company]
[Address]
[City, State ZIP]

Dear [Mr./Ms. Last Name]:

Thanks for your call. Enclosed please find the brochure that you requested. This brochure should answer most of your questions about [Products]. If you have any questions that it does not answer, certainly give me a call.

[Company Name] is proud of our products and we are certain you will be satisfied with our quality, installation, and customer service.

We look forward to adding you to that family of satisfied customers! I will call you in two weeks to follow up on where you are in your decision-making process and help you choose which of the [Products] you think might work best in your office.

Sincerely,

[Your Name]
[Your Address, if not on letterhead]

If someone takes the trouble to request a brochure, he or she is up there on the "serious potential customer" scale. Let your brochure do the initial talking, but always indicate in a cover letter that you plan to follow up.

Confirmation Letter 4

[Date]

[Name]
[Company]
[Address]
[City, State ZIP]

Dear [Mr./Ms. Last Name]:

I am writing to confirm from our phone conversation that you would like to upgrade our cleaning service agreement from once a month to once a week. Congratulations that your business has surpassed your expectations!

I am pleased that you are happy with our service and I have passed along your compliments to the team that cleans your establishment. We work hard to hire people who share our high standards for serving our customers.

Enclosed you will find a new service agreement. Please sign both copies, return one to us, and keep the other for your files. The agreement also outlines the new services you have chosen—window washing and plant watering. If anything in the agreement does not reflect what we discussed, please call and we will send you a revised agreement immediately.

As usual, I am just a phone call away. As the saying goes, if you have complaints, please call me; if you have compliments, please be sure to tell your friends!

Sincerely,

[Your Name]
[Your Address, if not on letterhead]

Always confirm any changes in a service contract and have the customer sign a new service agreement. And always be sure to acknowledge a business that is thriving—keeping any size business is hard work and customers will appreciate your recognition of their success and your compliments!

Confirmation Letter 5

[Date]

[Name]
[Company]
[Address]
[City, State ZIP]

Dear [Mr./Ms. Last Name]:

We are looking forward to catering your company's anniversary reception on [Day] evening [Date].

Here are the details we discussed:

- an estimated 200 people will attend
- the first cocktail will be compliments of the company, using a ticket you will provide at the door; the remaining drinks will be on a cash basis
- we will provide a DJ from 8 pm to 10 pm
- our staff will wander the floor with hors d'oeuvres trays from 7 pm to 9 pm (see food list attached)
- we will clean up all of our equipment and take leftover food with us

You will find a food list attached. Please approve this list by signing at the bottom and returning it to us with a deposit check in the amount of $500 by [Date].

Thank you for your business!

Sincerely,

[Your Name]
[Your Address, if not on letterhead]

Use bulleted lists to make the important details easier to find and read.

Thank-You Letter 1

If you are enclosing an evaluation or a survey that you want people to complete and return by mail, be sure to point out that it is already addressed and stamped. When customers know upfront that it is as easy as sticking a postcard or an envelope in the mail, they are more likely to do as you're requesting.

[Date]

[Name]
[Company]
[Address]
[City, State ZIP]

Dear [Mr./Ms. Last Name]:

Thank you for choosing [Company Name] to service your vehicle. We are proud of our service record and are always striving to better meet our customers' needs.

With that in mind, I am hoping you will take the time to fill out the enclosed service evaluation card. The card is self-addressed and stamped, so you can just pop it into the mail.

We take your comments seriously and are eager to address any concerns you may have had about your service. And of course, we appreciate any compliments!

We look forward to serving you the next time your vehicle needs repair or maintenance.

Sincerely,

[Your Name]
[Your Address, if not on letterhead]

Thanks-You Letter 2

[Date]

[Name]
[Company]
[Address]
[City, State ZIP]

Dear [Mr./Ms. Last Name]:

[Company Name] appreciated the recent opportunity to be able to service [New Customer's Name]'s vehicle. We are proud of our work and new customers quickly become loyal customers.

We want to thank you for sending [New Customer's Name] to us. In appreciation, we are enclosing a card for 10% off your next visit with us.

Everyone at [Company Name] understands that our current customers are most valuable in helping us help new customers. There are a lot of repair shops out there and we know how hard we need to work to keep your business. And we're happy to do it.

Sincerely,

[Your Name]
[Your Address, if not on letterhead]

Using actual names in letters like this makes a much greater impression on customers. Do it whenever you can.

Thank-You Letter 3

Sending a gift certificate for something besides a discount at your own company is a nice gesture, especially when it spreads the wealth to other local businesses.

[Date]

[Name]
[Company]
[Address]
[City, State ZIP]

Dear [Mr./Ms. Last Name]:

[Company Name] Insurance Company is proud to have insured you for over 30 years. Your excellent driving record has helped us keep your insurance costs down, a situation that makes us both happy!

With so many insurance companies, including nationwide chains advertising on national television, we know you have many other choices for your insurance needs. We especially appreciate that you chose a local company and have continued to choose to trust us.

In appreciation for your loyalty to our company and your good driving record, we are sending you the enclosed gift certificate to [Restaurant Name]. We entertain clients there and know you will enjoy Chef [Name]'s superb menu.

Again, thank you for your years of business and we look forward to serving you in the future.

Sincerely,

[Your Name]
[Your Address, if not on letterhead]

Response to Complaint 1

[Date]

[Name]
[Company]
[Address]
[City, State ZIP]

Dear [Mr./Ms. Last Name]:

Thank you for your recent letter. We are sorry you had a bad experience with our vending machine. We thought we had remedied this problem, but since you have brought it to our attention, we realize the problem still exists. Our service unit is back on the task of addressing this issue.

In the meantime, we are recalling all of our vending machines that use this delivery mechanism. We will replace them with others until we get the matter solved.

Our local sales representative will be contacting you within the next week to schedule pickup of the defective machine and delivery of a replacement.

Again, thank you for calling this matter to our attention. We are sorry for any inconvenience this has caused you.

Sincerely,

[Your Name]
[Your Address, if not on letterhead]

Never make light of a customer's complaint or put the blame elsewhere. Just own up to the responsibility of the problem and explain what you are going to do for the customer.

Response to Complaint 2

[Date]

[Name]
[Company]
[Address]
[City, State ZIP]

Dear [Mr./Ms. Last Name]:

Thank you for writing regarding the problem you have with the packaging of [Product Name]. While we understand that the box is a little more tightly sealed and therefore takes a little more effort to open, we felt we needed to make the compromise in convenience to address the complaints from our major retailers that the boxes were allowing crumbs to leak out.

We are pleased to enclose a supply of coupons as a small compensation for your frustration. Please know that we are always reevaluating our products and will keep your comments in mind when we review the packaging of [Product Name].

Sincerely,

[Your Name]
[Your Address, if not on letterhead]

You can say that you aren't able to do anything about a customer's complaint in the nicest way possible!

Response to Complaint 3

[Date]

[Name]
[Company]
[Address]
[City, State ZIP]

Dear [Mr./Ms. Last Name]:

Thank you for your recent correspondence. I am sorry you had a negative experience with one of our employees. Let me assure you not only that this is the exception at [Company Name] but also that we take these matters seriously. Our customers are of top importance to us.

I have spoken with [Mr./Ms. Last Name]. [He/She] assured me [He/She] realizes that this is in no way the approach we take with our customers. This was [His/Her] first time in the office alone, while the rest of us were out attending a trade show. [He/She] did not know how to appropriately respond to your concerns about the timing of your delivery.

We are making note of this interaction in [His/Her] personnel file in the unlikely event that a complaint such as yours arises again. And we are making sure that we train our employees to handle these kinds of unexpected situations appropriately.

For all future concerns, I invite you to contact me directly. As President of [Company Name], I will make sure that your concerns are addressed in a timely manner and with the utmost courtesy and respect.

We continue to appreciate your business.

Sincerely,

[Your Name]
[Your Address, if not on letterhead]

Make sure your complaint response letters include exactly what you are doing to correct the problem. You don't have to tell your customers everything, but you must let them know that you take their complaints seriously.

Response to Complaint 4

[Date]

[Name]
[Company]
[Address]
[City, State ZIP]

Dear [Mr./Ms. Last Name]:

I am very sorry to hear that you did not like our product, [Product Name]. We appreciate your taking the time to write to us and let us know specifically what you didn't like.

Enclosed you will find a refund check for the entire cost of your purchase, along with the shipping charges that you paid when ordering it and reimbursement of your expense for shipping it back to us.

We take these matters seriously and will be sure to consider your complaints in an upcoming review of our [Product Name].

Sincerely,

[Your Name]
[Your Address, if not on letterhead]

You can often keep disgruntled customers if you respond promptly to their concerns and assure them that you are taking their complaints into consideration.

Response to Complaint 5

[Date]

[Name]
[Company]
[Address]
[City, State ZIP]

Dear [Mr./Ms. Last Name]:

I received your phone call regarding the item missing from the fax machine you received from us recently. The machine is manufactured in China. We do not keep a supply of this particular part. Therefore, we are offering you a choice.

You could keep the machine and wait for the part to reach us and for us to send it to you immediately. This would take four to six weeks. Meanwhile, you could be using the machine, since the part is not critical to operation. Or, if you prefer, we could send you a replacement machine, which you would receive within the next five business days, and we would send a courier to retrieve the one with the missing part.

Please let us know which solution you prefer, using the enclosed addressed, stamped postcard. We appreciate your business and we apologize for the inconvenience.

Sincerely,

[Your Name]
[Your Address, if not on letterhead]

It might seem that you could handle this matter with phone calls, but it is often best to use written correspondence to create a paper trail when resolving this kind of complaint.

Follow-up Letter 1

[Date]

[Name]
[Company]
[Address]
[City, State ZIP]

Dear [Mr./Ms. Last Name]:

Enclosed is the material you requested about [Subject]. [Company Name] has done considerable research on this topic and we are proud to offer it for your review.

I would like to call you on [Date] and talk with you about [Subject] after you have read the material. I would particularly like to know if it was helpful to you and if you have any questions or things you think we should add to our research.

Again, thanks for contacting us. I will be calling you [Date].

Sincerely,

[Your Name]
[Your Address, if not on letterhead]

Use follow-up letters to notify people that you plan to call them and what you would like to discuss. This allows them to better prepare for your call.

Follow-up Letter 2

[Date]

[Name]
[Company]
[Address]
[City, State ZIP]

Dear [Mr./Ms. Last Name]:

In [Month], we sent you a replacement fax machine. I am writing to inquire if this resolution to your problem went smoothly and if you are happy with your new machine.

Enclosed you will find a customer satisfaction survey that I hope you will take the time to fill out and return. We take customer complaints very seriously and want to be sure we are satisfying our customers to the very best of our ability. I have also enclosed a coupon for your next purchase, in appreciation for completing the survey.

Sincerely,

[Your Name]
[Your Address, if not on letterhead]

Follow-up Letter 3

[Date]

[Name]
[Company]
[Address]
[City, State ZIP]

Dear [Mr./Ms. Last Name]:

I was delighted to get your letter regarding how much you enjoyed using [Product Name]. We are very proud of [Product Name] and are pleased with the positive response we are getting from people like you.

The marketing department is working on a new marketing campaign for [Product Name] to allow us to reach more people with this important product. We were hoping you might give us permission to use some of the comments from your letter as testimonials in our marketing efforts.

If you agree to this, please sign and return the enclosed consent form, using the self-addressed, stamped envelope. As the form states, we assure you that your comments will be printed exactly as they appeared in your letter.

We've also enclosed a discount coupon toward your next purchase of our product, as a small token of our appreciation.

Sincerely,

[Your Name]
[Your Address, if not on letterhead]

Consent forms are important. Make sure your cover letter explains how you plan to use the customer's words and that you do not plan to alter them. And, as always when you ask someone to return something, enclose a self-addressed, stamped envelope.

Credit Request Letter

[Date]

[Name]
[Company]
[Address]
[City, State ZIP]

Dear [Mr./Ms. Last Name]:

My store, [Store Name], has been doing business with you on a cash basis since we opened 18 months ago. In that time, we have placed six orders. I am writing now to ask you to set up an account for us.

We expect to be doing a similar amount of business with you over the next 18 months. We would like to set up an account with a credit limit of [Amount] and terms of 30 days from invoice. Then, in 18 months we would review our purchasing to see if this limit and these terms are still appropriate.

I appreciate your prompt reply and look forward to many years of doing business with you.

Sincerely,

[Your Name]
[Your Address, if not on letterhead]

Be specific about the credit terms you want. You may not get them, but if you are reasonable, you probably will. If not, you at least express your expectations so the company does not set you up with terms much lower than you wanted.

Credit Letter

[Date]

[Name]
[Company]
[Address]
[City, State ZIP]

Dear [Mr./Ms. Last Name]:

We appreciate your business these past 18 months and are pleased to offer [Company Name] an account. The terms you requested, [Amount] credit limit and 30 days from invoice terms, are acceptable to us. We will be happy to review the account again in 18 months at your request.

Although we have your purchasing record with us, we also request three other credit references in order to set up an account. If you could provide us with those, we will get your account in place as soon as possible.

Again, thanks very much for your business!

Sincerely,

[Your Name]
[Your Address, if not on letterhead]

Always get credit references, even with a company that has been doing cash business with you. When extending credit, you can never do enough to reduce your risk.

Collections Letter 1

[Date]

[Name]
[Company]
[Address]
[City, State ZIP]

Dear [Mr./Ms. Last Name]:

Our records show that you have a past due balance of [Amount]. If you have sent a check already, please accept our thanks.

If not, perhaps you have simply overlooked this matter. We would appreciate it if you would send a check immediately. We appreciate your business and want you to remain a customer in good standing with [Company Name].

Sincerely,

[Your Name]
[Your Address, if not on letterhead]

Always start the collections process with a friendly reminder. But don't wait too long to send this letter and then, if you do not receive payment, don't wait too long to send the next level of reminder, which isn't quite so friendly.

Collections Letter 2

Point out exactly the negative results when a customer fails to pay. Give the customer one last opportunity to contact you about payment plans. A completely unresponsive customer is sign of serious financial problems and you should not delay in taking action to get your overdue payment.

[Date]

[Name]
[Company]
[Address]
[City, State ZIP]

Dear [Mr./Ms. Last Name]:

Despite several reminders, the last on [Date], about the unpaid balance on your account, we have not yet received payment. Please send the amount due of [Amount] immediately. If you are unable to send the payment immediately, please contact me with a date of when you will send payment.

We do as much as we can to help customers through tough financial situations, but unfortunately, our next course of action is to send your account to collections, which means that your account will be closed and a negative notation be put on your credit report. We would prefer to avoid taking that step and we are sure you would not want to force us to do so.

Sincerely,

[Your Name]
[Your Address, if not on letterhead]

## Chapter 11

Business-to-Business Purchasing Letters

All companies do lots of business not only with their customers but also with other businesses. You order supplies, sign contracts for services, compliment and complain about services and products, refuse shipments, and express appreciation.

These letters by which you do these things are an important part of keeping your business running smoothly and efficiently. Maintaining your business-to-business relationships and seeking out new relationships is all part of doing business—and doing it well.

Keep these letters brief and professional. If you know a recipient personally, it is great to add a line or two of personal information (such as "How are the kids?"). Don't forget, however, that these letters become part of the record of your business operation. You don't need to write with serious formality, but don't get too involved in personal matters and don't bury the point of your letters.

You will be creating B2B letters for the following purposes:

- asking to set up an account and for credit terms
- ordering goods and materials and confirming your orders
- making service agreements
- refusing shipments you didn't order or that come in substandard
- complaining about poor quality (don't forget to send a few quality compliment letters too!)
- thanking people for good service, terms that helped you make a good deal, fast turnaround times, and so on

Vendors expect you to expect quality service. Don't expect them to read your mind: if you are unhappy with services or products, it is your responsibility to let your vendors know. Since many vendors don't use their products or services, they may never know about problems unless their customers tell them.

But don't be a pest, either. A squeaky wheel sometimes gets the grease, but if it continues to squeak, people will eventually just ignore it. Be sure your complaints are valid. Start off by giving your vendor the benefit of the doubt. Reputable vendors do not want to sell inferior products or provide inferior services. They want you to be happy with what they're selling because their business depends on your business.

If you don't get the satisfaction you want, but you still prefer to do business with the vendor, you will need to make your complaints stronger. You will probably start off talking with the vendor on the phone. Then, if the call fails to resolve the issue, write a letter. A letter also provides documentation that you have gone through a formal complaint process before you take the step of deciding not to pay for goods or services you consider substandard.

Credit Check

[Date]

[Name]
[Company]
[Address]
[City, State ZIP]

Dear [Mr./Ms. Last Name]:

[Company Name] has requested to open an account with us. Your company's name was provided as a credit reference. Could you please take a moment to answer the following questions and return this letter to me in the stamped, self-addressed envelope provided? These answers will remain confidential. Thanks for your time.

- Does [Company Name] have a current account with you?

- How long has [Company Name] done business with your company?

- What is their average monthly balance on account?

- Do they pay their invoices and statements on time?

- Have you ever had to send their account to collections?

- Do you consider them a good credit risk?

Sincerely,

[Your Name]
[Your Address, if not on letterhead]

Don't expect people to answer questions you don't ask. If you want an answer to something, ask it point-blank.

Credit Letter

[Date]

[Name]
[Company]
[Address]
[City, State ZIP]

Dear [Mr./Ms. Last Name]:

We are pleased to inform you that we have established an account for [Company Name]. The account credit limit is [Amount], which we will be happy to reassess six months from now. Invoices will be due 30 days from the date on the invoice. Your account is now open; you may use it immediately upon receipt of this letter.

Your account number is [Number]. Please be sure to include your account number on all correspondence with us.

We appreciate your desire to do business with us and look forward to helping your company meet its financial goals and its customers' needs.

Sincerely,

[Your Name]
[Your Address, if not on letterhead]

Even as you are providing a benefit to the other company by extending credit, you are receiving a benefit in the new account, so you should be sure to express your appreciation.

Credit Rejection

[Date]

[Name]
[Company]
[Address]
[City, State ZIP]

Dear [Mr./Ms. Last Name]:

Thank you for asking [Company Name] about opening an account. Unfortunately, your company's credit history does not make it possible for us to extend credit to [Other Company's Name] at this time.

We understand you are trying to rebuild your business after going through some rough years and we would truly like to help you. Please know that this decision is not final; we would be happy to reassess our decision in six months, after you have had been able to place some orders with us and pay cash and reestablish good credit elsewhere as well.

Thank you for considering [Company Name] as a supplier. We wish you the best in your rebuilding effort and we look forward to doing business with you.

Sincerely,

[Your Name]
[Your Address, if not on letterhead]

You can and should certainly be sympathetic and help a customer rebuild credit, but you should not feel apologetic about minimizing credit risks to your company.

Initial Order

[Date]

[Name]
[Company]
[Address]
[City, State ZIP]

Dear [Mr./Ms. Last Name]:

I am opening a retail gift store on [Street] called [Store Name]. Our store is scheduled to open on [Date].

I have attached an initial order. Please let me know whether everything I have ordered is in stock and when I might expect to receive the order. I am planning to have the store stocked and ready in time for our grand opening [Date].

At some point I would like to set up an account with [Company Name]. Please let me know what steps I need to take to do that and if there are minimum quantities I would need to order.

Sincerely,

[Your Name]
[Your Address, if not on letterhead]

Most vendors require that initial orders from new stores be paid in cash. However, don't hesitate to initiate the process of getting an account as soon as possible.

Request for Estimate

[Date]

[Name]
[Company]
[Address]
[City, State ZIP]

Dear [Mr./Ms. Last Name]:

[Store Name] is adding catalog sales to our successful retail operation. I am writing to request a quote for printing our catalog. Here are the specifications, which are subject to change; your estimate will help us make final decisions. We are open to suggestions about any of our specs:

- print cycle twice per year to start
- four-color process printing
- self cover
- approximately 64 pages
- approximately four photos per page, totaling around 200, provided digitally on CD
- ship all to our warehouse in [City], [State]
- print run: please quote 10,000/15,000/25,000

We have been in business for five years and we have good credit references that we can provide to set up an account with your company. We would hope to pay in three stages, 1/3 upfront, 1/3 on delivery, and 1/3 within 30 days of delivery. This would mean that we would always pay off the balance on a catalog before beginning the next catalog.

We would greatly appreciate receiving your estimate as soon as possible. Please contact me directly if you need more information.

Sincerely,

[Your Name]

[Your Address, if not on letterhead]

If you have credit references, by all means try to get terms on your first order. Suggest a reasonable payment schedule that you prefer; you never know what you might get if you ask!

Order Verification

Lots of orders are taken over the phone. Backing it up with a letter of verification is important—it would be expensive to send a big shipment for which delivery is then refused because no one had confirmed the order and the organization had decided meanwhile to order a product from another company.

[Date]

[Name]
[Company]
[Address]
[City, State ZIP]

Dear [Mr./Ms. Last Name]:

Thank you for your phone call yesterday requesting 2,000 of our [Product] for your [Name] Festival. This letter serves to verify this order and the terms we agreed on.

You will take receipt of this order at the Festival headquarters, [Address], on [Date]. We will send the order COD. We will accept return of unused [Products], up to a maximum of 10 percent (or 200) of the order.

Please sign the bottom of this letter and return it to me in the self-addressed, stamped envelope enclosed. Be sure to keep a copy for yourself.

Thank you for your order. I wish you the best of luck with the Festival!

Sincerely,

[Your Name]
[Your Address, if not on letterhead]

Service Agreement Letter

[Date]

[Name]
[Company]
[Address]
[City, State ZIP]

Dear [Mr./Ms. Last Name]:

Thank you for choosing [Company Name] for your company's landscaping maintenance service. We are confident that you will join our long list of satisfied customers. We enjoyed touring your grounds—your landscape designer did a great job of thinking ahead for making your property efficient to maintain!

We are enclosing a formal service agreement; you should sign and return it to us well before the first day of service on [Date]. Our team will be at your facility every Friday. Please alert us by Thursday morning of any special requests so that the team will be sure to bring the supplies and equipment they will need.

Highlights of what we are providing in our service include:

- mowing all lawns on the grounds
- replanting the flower beds in the spring, summer, and fall
- applying fresh mulch twice annually, spring and fall
- weeding and watering flower beds and replacing plants when necessary
- trimming hedges and shrubs twice annually
- keeping tree limbs trimmed enough to not dangle over parked cars
- cleaning up after any significant storm damage
- trimming weeds and grass along building edges

We will alert you of course to any damage we see on buildings, the parking lot, or the walkways as we do our maintenance work.

Thank you so much for choosing [Company Name]. We truly appreciate your business.

Sincerely,

[Your Name]
[Your Title]
[Your Address, if not on letterhead]

Most people don't read service agreements in detail, so in your cover letter be sure to point out highlights of the agreement. And always compliment the company if you can.

Service Agreement Letter 1

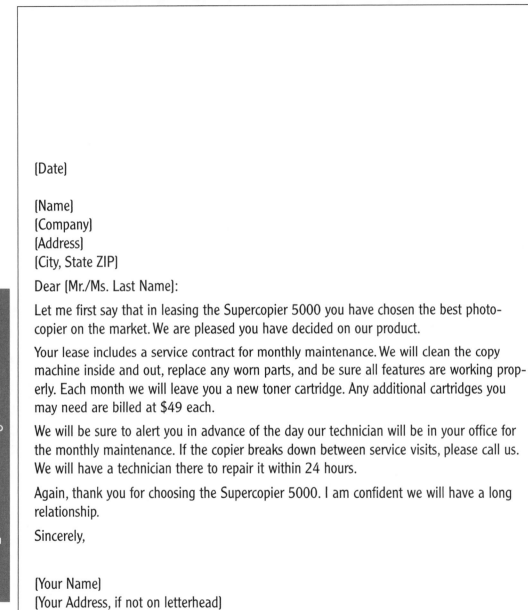

The lease may have spelled out the maintenance agreement, but sometimes the details get lost in the legal verbiage, so it is good customer relations to point out benefits like maintenance. And there is no better time to establish good customer relations as when you start doing business with a customer!

[Date]

[Name]
[Company]
[Address]
[City, State ZIP]

Dear [Mr./Ms. Last Name]:

Let me first say that in leasing the Supercopier 5000 you have chosen the best photo-copier on the market. We are pleased you have decided on our product.

Your lease includes a service contract for monthly maintenance. We will clean the copy machine inside and out, replace any worn parts, and be sure all features are working prop-erly. Each month we will leave you a new toner cartridge. Any additional cartridges you may need are billed at $49 each.

We will be sure to alert you in advance of the day our technician will be in your office for the monthly maintenance. If the copier breaks down between service visits, please call us. We will have a technician there to repair it within 24 hours.

Again, thank you for choosing the Supercopier 5000. I am confident we will have a long relationship.

Sincerely,

[Your Name]
[Your Address, if not on letterhead]

Service Agreement Letter 2

[Date]

[Name]
[Company]
[Address]
[City, State ZIP]

Dear [Mr./Ms. Last Name]:

We are pleased you want to renew your agreement with us for delivery service for [Florist Company Name].

In the four years that we have worked together, we have kept our prices low; we have raised our prices only once. Unfortunately, the escalating price of fuel is forcing us to increase our prices, as I mentioned when we talked, starting with the beginning of the new agreement, effective [Date], an increase that you will see reflected in item 6 on the enclosed agreement. Otherwise, our lease agreement remains essentially the same.

We have worked hard to find ways to cut costs so we can keep our price increase to a minimum, including a new fleet of more fuel-efficient vehicles. We appreciate your understanding; if you have any ideas for helping keep costs down, we are open to hearing them!

We have enjoyed working with you and look forward to another year of good business for us both.

Sincerely,

[Your Name]
[Your Address, if not on letterhead]

Don't get too apologetic about price increases, but be sure to give a brief explanation and point out if you have not raised your prices in a few years.

Service Agreement Estimate Request Letter

[Date]

[Name]
[Company]
[Address]
[City, State ZIP]

Dear [Mr./Ms. Last Name]:

Please provide us with an estimate for grounds maintenance services for our two proper-ties, located at [Address 1] and [Address 2] in [City]. We would like the following services:

- mowing all lawns on the grounds (twice a month)
- keeping lawns weed-free and applying pesticides, herbicides, and fungicides as needed
- replanting the flower beds in the spring, summer, and fall
- applying fresh mulch twice annually, spring and fall
- weeding and watering flower beds and replacing plants when necessary
- trimming hedges and shrubs twice annually
- keeping tree limbs trimmed enough to not dangle over parked cars
- cleaning up after any significant storm damage
- trimming weeds and grass along building edges

If, after viewing the properties, you have further questions, please feel free to call me at the number on this letterhead. I would appreciate your estimate within two weeks.

Thank you.

Sincerely,

[Your Name]
[Your Address, if not on letterhead]

Whenever you request an estimate for anything, always ask at least three vendors. Be sure you ask each for the exact same services so you are comparing apples with apples when you make your decision.

Letter Refusing Shipment 1

[Date]

[Name]
[Company]
[Address]
[City, State ZIP]

Dear [Mr./Ms. Last Name]:

We received a pallet of books today via [Carrier] with the shipping number [Number]. The boxes looked damaged, both stained (apparently from getting wet) and dented. We opened one box and, in fact, most of the books were water-damaged and some were bent and crushed.

We have hundreds of back orders that we were hoping to fill with this shipment. Please let us know how soon you can have this shipment replaced so we can give our customers a date by which they can expect to receive their orders.

We are discouraged, of course. However, we have always had excellent service from you and understand that problems like this happen on occasion. We know you will help us with a prompt response to this problem.

Sincerely,

[Your Name]
[Your Address, if not on letterhead]

Stuff happens. Unless problems occur regularly, there is no need to get an attitude about them. Of course, your company loses money and time, but instead of getting angry you should focus your energy on getting your vendors to respond appropriately. If they do not, then you should use your energy to find new vendors.

Letter Refusing Shipment 2

A serious problem with a vendor, especially one that has not proven itself to you, may call for a serious solution. Cut your losses and drop the vendor from your list. And let them know point-blank that you don't intend to do future business with them.

[Date]

[Name]
[Address]
[City, State ZIP]

Dear [Mr./Ms. Last Name]:

We have just refused shipment on an order of 1,000 candles that we placed six weeks ago. We needed to receive the candles from you by 6/1 for an event scheduled for 6/4. They did not arrive here by 6/2. We called your customer service line, but we got no satisfaction. We decided that we had no choice but to go elsewhere, to drive to [City] and purchase candles at the [Company Name] discount warehouse.

Please cancel our order. Also, we no longer need to see your sales representative.

Sincerely,

[Your Name]
[Your Address, if not on letterhead]

Leeter Refusing Shipment 3

[Date]

[Name]
[Company]
[Address]
[City, State ZIP]

Dear [Mr./Ms. Last Name]:

We received a puzzling shipment from your warehouse today that we had to refuse. The shipping receipt said the shipment included 10,000 rubber ducks. We did not order 10,000 rubber ducks; in fact, we have not placed an order with your company for several months.

A call to your customer service revealed that this shipment should have gone to [Company Name] across town on West Road, not to our company on West Highway. Your customer service representative was planning to call [Company Name] to let them know the shipment was being redirected.

Since this error meant only a minor inconvenience for the customer and for you, I guess we can all get a little chuckle out of this. We were surprised to find 10,000 rubber ducks at our loading dock! Thankfully, they did not get out of the boxes before we discovered the error.

Sincerely,

[Your Name]
[Your Address, if not on letterhead]

Sometimes things are just funny. A letter like this can be faxed to the company so they know immediately, in writing, that the shipment is on the way to the right location. A phone call is important too, but a follow-up letter documents the situation, to dispel any confusion about what happened and how it was resolved.

Quality Complaint 1

[Date]

[Name]
[Company]
[Address]
[City, State ZIP]

Dear [Mr./Ms. Last Name]:

You fulfilled and delivered our order for personalized ink pens in a timely fashion. The engraving looks great and everything was spelled correctly, which has been a problem at times with our unusual name.

Unfortunately, the pens seem to be very inferior in quality. Many of the built-in flashlights do not work and the pen retractors break easily.

We are extremely disappointed with this product. We would like to return this shipment and order a simpler pen that is less likely to break. Can you call me to discuss a new order and what we can do about this shipment? We have a trade show in three weeks and we had planned to hand out pens at our booth, so we would appreciate it if you respond promptly.

Sincerely,

[Your Name]
[Your Address, if not on letterhead]

Don't just put up with inferior products. Don't accept them. Ask the company to figure out how to make good on the order.

Quality Complaint 2

[Date]

[Name]
[Company]
[Address]
[City, State ZIP]

Dear [Mr./Ms. Last Name]:

We have several boxes of riding tights that we ordered from you for last summer that never sold. Customers who tried them on complained that the stitching was too tight along the reinforcement in the leg, causing wrinkling all down the leg. This is unacceptable for showing, so they chose not to purchase them.

We request that you either allow us to return the remaining stock to you or give us a substantial additional discount so that we can reduce the price enough to sell them as schooling britches or perhaps on eBay.

I can be reached at the number at the top of this letter. Thank you for your prompt attention to this matter.

Sincerely,

[Your Name]
[Your Address, if not on letterhead]

Sometimes returning product can be very inefficient. Suggest alternatives that make it less work for you. You never know what a company will be willing to accept. And you can assume that a product that's a problem for you has probably generated other complaints, so the company may have already figured out a solution.

Quality Complaint 3

Sometimes it just takes a simple letter to get something turned around and running smoothly again. You could do this over the phone, and perhaps you should make a phone call in addition to sending a letter, but it is always best to put a complaint in writing.

[Date]

[Name]
[Company]
[Address]
[City, State ZIP]

Dear [Mr./Ms. Last Name]:

We have had a service contract with your landscape maintenance company for almost seven years. We have had no reason to complain until six months ago, when you hired a new team manager for our site.

Now, employees are routinely reporting that grass clippings are left on the walkway, tools are in places where they could cause injury or damage, your workers are sitting on our front curb and smoking, and maintenance vehicles and machines are blocking employee vehicles. These are problems we never experienced with previous team managers.

I would appreciate if you would talk with your manager about proper conduct on the clients' premises. We have enjoyed doing business with you over most of the past seven years and would like that relationship to continue with the high standards we had come to expect.

Sincerely,

[Your Name]
[Your Address, if not on letterhead]

Service Complaint

[Date]

[Name]
[Company]
[Address]
[City, State ZIP]

Dear [Mr./Ms. Last Name]:

Our employees take their company cars to your dealership for routine service such as oil changes or for unexpected repairs. Several employees have reported that every time they go to your dealership for a simple oil change, someone from the service department tells them that the vehicle is in need of some repair that will cost $300-$400.

All of our employees are instructed to refuse to agree to these suggested repairs, unless the repairs are related to their reason for visiting the dealership. We find it interesting that the cars have continued to operate very well without these repairs.

We have concluded that your service department is suggesting unnecessary repairs. Please be advised that if this practice continues we will take our business to another dealership.

Sincerely,

[Your Name]
[Your Address, if not on letterhead]

Don't just complain behind the scenes. Call companies onto the carpet for issues you feel are hurting your business with them. Be sure to tell them you will take your business elsewhere. In instances like this one, sometimes employees in the department in question are the only people in the company who know what's happening. You don't want to abandon a business simply because of a specific problem that could be resolved if you complain.

Thank-You Letter 1

It is always good to follow up a complaint letter with a thank-you and acknowledgment that your complaint has been satisfactorily addressed. This is important because you may need to report problems in the future and you don't want people in the company to label you as a complainer and possibly ignore or dismiss your concerns. You want to show that you appreciate their efforts to resolve

[Date]

[Name]
[Company]
[Address]
[City, State ZIP]

Dear [Mr./Ms. Last Name]:

Thank you for taking care of my recent complaint regarding the decline in the conduct of the landscape team taking care of our office site.

We are happy to report that over the last month things have gone much more smoothly and the team members have been conducting themselves according to the high standard we had come to expect from your company. The team manager sought me out to apologize for the problems and to assure me that they won't happen again.

We look forward to continuing our relationship with your company.

Sincerely,

[Your Name]
[Your Address, if not on letterhead]

Thank-You Letter 2

[Date]

[Name]
[Company]
[Address]
[City, State ZIP]

Dear [Mr./Ms. Last Name]:

Please extend our thanks to all members of the [Hotel Name] staff for helping us run our recent conference without a hitch.

At the end, when we asked the participants to evaluate the conference, their responses all praised the excellent food and service as well as the cleanliness of your establishment.

Thank you all for helping to make our conference a success.

Sincerely,

[Your Name]
[Your Address, if not on letterhead]

Expressing appreciation is always a good way to have the staff look forward to working with you again.

Thank-You Letter 3

When people work hard and disrupt their lives at work and even at home when you travel to visit their location, be sure to acknowledge that effort and let them know you appreciated what they did to make you feel welcome.

[Date]

[Name]
[Company]
[Address]
(City, State ZIP)

Dear [Mr./Ms. Last Name]:

Thank you so much for your hospitality to my team members and me while we were staying in Denver to work on the project. We look forward to reciprocating when you visiting us in [City] in [Month].

Sincerely,

[Your Name]
[Your Address, if not on letterhead]

Personnel Letters

Most personnel letters will become part of an employee's permanent file. When reporting something negative, you need to be direct but tactful in your letter. When you're writing about something positive, it will help the employee if you make very clear your reason for writing the letter.

A letter that praises an employee for exceeding expectations or doing an exceptional job on an important project is important to the employee because it will filed as part of a record of his or her abilities and accomplishments.

A letter that reprimands an employee is important to an employer as legal documentation of attempts to remedy the problem, especially if the employee is fired at some point. Firing an employee requires following very specific tactics; documentation of the employer's dissatisfaction with the employee's performance is critical in avoiding legal action or at least in prevailing.

Firing an employee is a serious legal matter. You should always write a letter of termination of employment as well as talking with the employee. This letter should be to the point—nothing extra is necessary or desired. Simply state that employment is being terminated, briefly explain why, indicate when the termination is effective, outline the procedure for leaving the premises, and get a signature from the appropriate upper-level manager(s).

Receipt of Resume

[Date]

[Name]
[Company]
[Address]
[City, State ZIP]

Dear [Mr./Ms. Last Name]:

Thank you for sending your resume in application for our opening for [Position].

We are collecting resumes for this position until [Date]. At that time, we will begin our initial review of applications. The ones we determine to best fit the position will be passed along to a hiring committee to schedule interviews.

After [Date], we will contact you to let you know whether or not your application will be among those that the hiring committee considers. In the meantime, we appreciate your interest in [Company Name].

Sincerely,

[Your Name]
[Your Address, if not on letterhead]

It is very uncommon these days for companies to respond to resumes. However, if you solicit applications, it is a courtesy to respond at least with a form letter to let applicants know how the process works.

Response to Application

[Date]

[Name]
[Company]
[Address]
[City, State ZIP]

Dear [Mr./Ms. Last Name]:

We have received your resume and application for the position of [Position Title] as we advertised in the [Newspaper Title]. Your qualifications are excellent, and we have added you to the group of applicants we would like to bring in for interviews.

We are not quite ready to set up those interviews. Because we see this as a key position for the growth of our company, we are being extremely careful in our selection process. We will be in touch within the next two weeks to set up a phone interview. After we finish that stage, we will begin to bring in semifinalists for an in-person interview.

We appreciate your patience and your interest in [Company Name]. We look forward to talking with you soon.

Sincerely,

[Your Name]
[Your Address, if not on letterhead]

Seeking a job these days can be frustrating. Most companies do not respond at all to applications. If you have advertised a job, the least you can do is be prepared to send out a form letter to each applicant. For any applicant you may be interested in interviewing, you want to reflect the atmosphere of your company in your hiring process.

Rejection 1

Letting applicants for a job know upfront about a strong in-house candidate lets them decide whether to keep pursuing the job or not. And it is a logical reason for not hiring applicants who are good matches for the job. Almost everyone appreciates a company that promotes from within.

[Date]

[Name]
[Company]
[Address]
[City, State ZIP]

Dear [Mr./Ms. Last Name]:

Thank you for your interest in the [Position] opening here at [Company Name] and for taking the time to come in and meet with us twice. We all very much enjoyed meeting you.

As we have said from the beginning, there is a strong in-house candidate for this position. We decided to open it up to the outside because we felt we wanted to make sure we were not missing out on a more qualified candidate. When the members of the hiring committee sat down to make our final decision, we ultimately decided that our in-house candidate is the best qualified for the job.

Again, we appreciate your interest in [Company Name] and wish you all the best in locating a position that uses your many talents and skills.

Sincerely,

[Your Name]
[Your Address, if not on letterhead]

Rejection 2

[Date]

[Name]
[Company]
[Address]
[City, State ZIP]

Dear [Mr./Ms. Last Name]:

Thank you for your interest in working with [Company Name]. We have conducted phone interviews with the six candidates we felt best matched for the position.

We now have narrowed our field down to two. While you are not among those two finalists, we really enjoyed speaking with you and want you to know that it was a difficult choice, as all six candidates had very strong qualifications. However, we decided that it was most important to hire someone who could be up and running quickly, which requires someone with experience in this industry.

We wish you the best in your job search. We encourage you to apply to [Company Name] again if another position opens. We will keep your resume on file for six months in case that situation arises.

Sincerely,

[Your Name]
[Your Address, if not on letterhead]

If you can honestly tell an applicant that you would have considered him or her further except for one criterion, then by all means say so and encourage the applicant to apply in the future. But don't say this in a rejection letter unless you mean it.

Checking References

[Date]

[Name]
[Company]
[Address]
[City, State ZIP]

Dear [Mr./Ms. Last Name]:

We are in the process of hiring for [Position Title] and have reduced the list of applicants to two finalists. Before we make our decision, we are checking their references.

[Applicant Name] gave your name as a reference.

I would like to call you later this week. In the meantime, here are some of the questions I hope you might be able to answer:

- How long did [Name] work for you and what was [His/Her] job title?
- Did [Name] report directly to you?
- What responsibilities did [Name] have?
- How are [His/Her] organizational skills?
- How did [He/She] interact with others? Did [He/She] gain experience working on a team? If so, how did that go?
- What is the most positive trait you can think of when you think of [Name]?
- What do you think [Name] needs to work further on improving?

I appreciate your time. I will plan to call you on Friday morning.

Sincerely,

[Your Name]
[Your Address, if not on letterhead]

Sometimes an applicant may give as references people who have not worked with that person for several years. While the references can still be useful, it is helpful to send them a letter to notify them that you will be calling and listing things to think about to prepare for your call.

Job Offer

[Date]

[Name]
[Company]
[Address]
[City, State ZIP]

Dear [Mr./Ms. Last Name]:

We are so pleased to offer you the position of [Position Title] with [Company Name]. Everyone here enjoyed meeting with you and we all feel you have a lot to offer our company.

The details as we discussed are as follows:

- [Position Title]
- $[Salary]
- [Number] vacation days, sick days, and personal days
- [Health and/or Dental and/or Disability and/or Life Insurances]
- [Hours]
- reporting to [Name]
- supervising [Titles]

We hope you are as excited about starting your new position as we are about welcoming you to [Company Name]. As soon as we hear that you are in agreement about the above details, we will prepare a letter of agreement for you to sign.

Sincerely,

[Your Name]
[Your Address, if not on letterhead]

Outline the details of employment in an offer letter before preparing the letter of agreement. That way if your new employee thinks of a detail that you forgot or negotiates anything different, you can prepare the agreement accordingly.

Welcome Letter

[Date]

[Name]
[Company]
[Address]
[City, State ZIP]

Dear [Mr./Ms. Last Name]:

Welcome to the [Company Name] team! We are looking forward to your first day here on March 8.

Please plan to arrive at 9:00 am and check in with [Name of Receptionist] at the front desk. [He/She] will show you your office and general areas—bathrooms, cafeteria, coat closet, etc. Feel free to start making a list of the things you will need to make your office as comfortable and efficient as possible.

I will let you settle in a little and come by around 10:00 to take you around for introductions. You will then have a half hour or so to get your bearings a little more before we head out to lunch with the other team leaders.

We have a meeting scheduled for 3:00 pm in which we hope to begin the initial plans to help you establish your team. This meeting shouldn't last more than a couple of hours—it may be the only day you get out of here by 5:00, so plan to enjoy it!

I look forward to seeing you on Monday.

Sincerely,

[Your Name]
[Your Address, if not on letterhead]

Performance Review, Positive

[Date]

[Name]
[Company]
[Address]
[City, State ZIP]

Dear [Mr./Ms. Last Name]:

Attached is the form outlining the results of your performance review from last week. As I noted in the review, we are extremely pleased with the progress you have made in the few months you have been with the company. Some of the highlights are:

- You have brought in six new clients in just eight months. That is a record for the company!

- The people who report to you are very productive and the morale in your department has improved tremendously.

- You contribute productively to meetings.

- You have found efficiencies to help make your department more profitable.

- You have jumped right in and helped at conferences and sales meetings.

I am pleased that you, too, are happy with your employment with [Company Name]. I look forward to future positive performance reviews.

Please sign the enclosed copy, keep a copy for yourself, and return the original so I can add it to your personnel file.

Sincerely,

[Your Name]
[Your Address, if not on letterhead]

> You don't have to reiterate everything that's on the review form, but it is nice to point out some of the highlights that show which things you value the most in that employee.

Performance Review, Negative

Unless the poor performance is a repeat performance, it is not necessary to get very harsh in your criticism. Be upfront about your disappointment and suggest ways for the employee to improve. Dejected employees are less likely to improve; however, those who know they have a champion in the company will be inspired to do better.

[Date]

[Name]
[Company]
[Address]
[City, State ZIP]

Dear [Mr./Ms. Last Name]:

This letter is to follow up on the difficult performance review we had last week. As we discussed, we are not pleased with the quality of the projects you are bringing to the table. Only one of your projects has sold well in the past year, and that performance was in great part because it is part of an established successful series.

I know you are aware of these issues. We discussed several ways that the company might help you perform better in your role as [Position Title], all of which are listed on the attached review form. Please be sure to start working on these recommendations and get the help you need. We agreed that you could spend some money on conferences and other gatherings that might put you in a position to find better projects.

Please sign the enclosed review indicating you have read it. Keep a copy for your own files and return the original to me for your personnel records.

We of course expect your performance to improve in the next year. I am confident you are capable of it and look forward to a positive review in [Year].

Sincerely,

[Your Name]
[Your Address, if not on letterhead]

Promotion 1

[Date]

[Name]
[Company]
[Address]
[City, State ZIP]

Dear [Mr./Ms. Last Name]:

Congratulations on your promotion to [Position Title]! We are always pleased to be able to promote our employees. With a performance like you have exhibited over the past three years, you really deserve this promotion.

Please let me know if there is anything that any of us can do to help you succeed in your new position. Don't forget: since this is a new position in the company, we will need to finalize your job description and get it to the HR department sometime in the next two weeks.

Sincerely,

[Your Name]
[Your Address, if not on letterhead]

Don't skimp on your congratulations—it's an easy way to emphasize something positive. If something needs to be completed, always give a timeline. People shouldn't be left wondering when to do something; most appreciate deadlines.

Promotion 2

It is good public relations to congratulate someone outside your company who may not be working with you anymore. This type of kindness goes a long way in ensuring that your company continues to be treated well. In this case, the new sales manager is likely to make it clear to your new sales rep to be particularly attentive to you.

[Date]

[Name]
[Company]
[Address]
[City, State ZIP]

Dear [Mr./Ms. Last Name]:

Congratulations on your recent promotion to sales manager. We have always appreciated your close attention to our account and your prompt response to any concerns we have had while you were our sales representative. While we will miss seeing you regularly, we feel confident we are in good hands with you managing sales for your company.

Best of luck! If you are ever in our area, please stop by for a visit.

Sincerely,

[Your Name]
[Your Address, if not on letterhead]

Termination 1

[Date]

[Name]
[Company]
[Address]
[City, State ZIP]

Dear [Mr./Ms. Last Name]:

The following information is in connection with your termination of employment with [Company Name], effective [Date]:

1. Your final check is paid through [Date], includes a vacation balance of [Number] [Days/Hours], and will be directly deposited into your bank account.

2. You will be receiving information on COBRA regarding continuation of our medical, dental, and life insurance, per government regulations.

3. You have [Number] months from [Date] to exercise your stock options. You are vested for [Number] of shares at [Price] per share. On the last page of your stock option agreement, you will find the form to fill out to exercise your stock options. Please see the stock option agreement for further details.

4. I have enclosed a copy of the confidentiality agreement that you signed when we hired you. You should read this over so that you do not unintentionally violate the terms of this agreement.

Sincerely,

[Your Name]
[Your Title]
[Your Address, if not on letterhead]

Termination should be quite formal. Outline anything of importance and remind the employee of any noncompete and confidentiality agreements.

Termination 2

[Date]

[Name]
[Company]
[Address]
[City, State ZIP]

Dear [Mr./Ms. Last Name]:

We are sorry to inform you that your employment with [Company Name] will be terminated effective [Date]. As we have discussed, the past two years you have performed poorly. It is standard company policy to terminate employees with poor performance reviews for two years running.

Please clean out your desk and files by the end of your last day. Turn your office keys in to the receptionist.

This letter will be followed by one from the HR department outlining the details of your final paycheck and other personnel matters.

I am sorry this hasn't worked out better. We wish you the best in your future endeavors.

Sincerely,

[Your Name]
[Your Address, if not on letterhead]

If an employee has tried hard but just hasn't worked out, there is no need to be abusive in your termination letter. Be clear about the details of termination, express your regrets, and let everyone begin to move on.

Recommendation 1

[Date]

[Name]
[Company]
[Address]
[City, State ZIP]

Dear [Mr./Ms. Last Name]:

I am very pleased to recommend [Name] to the position of [Title] at [Company Name].

[Name] worked here for five years, beginning in [Month/Year] and ending in [Month/Year]. [He/She] was a valued employee. [Name] got along very well with everyone and worked extremely hard in [His/Her] position.

As the point person for setting up our booth at the many trade shows that we attend, [Name] was organized and thought ahead about every possible thing we might need at the show. [He/She] is very assertive and could fix any problem that came up. Our booths were always neat and attractive and [he/she] thought of details, such as having bottled water on hand.

[Name] did all this cost-effectively and was able to find cost-efficiencies that allowed [him/her] to make booth salespeople comfortable, providing such things as cushioned flooring—knowing that a comfortable salesperson sells better! [Name] constantly searched for new ways to make our booth better, more effective, more comfortable, and easier to put up and break down.

[Name] was also good at teaching [his/her] employees, so we luckily were able to promote [his/her] assistant to take over when [Name] was away. When [Name] decided not to continue with us, we promoted [his/her] assistant to the position permanently.

[He/She] is a great employee and I would hire [him/her] back in a minute if we had a position available.

Sincerely,

[Your Name]
[Your Address, if not on letterhead]

Employers always like to know if you would hire the employee again if the opportunity arose.

Recommendation 2

If it has been a long time since an employee worked for you, keep your recommendation fairly general. Potential employees will appreciate your pointing out any issues with the employee, which is fine if they were resolved. As recommendations have been used in legal actions, more and more former employers have become reluctant to offer them. But if you can say some things with confidence, it shouldn't be a problem.

[Date]

[Name]
[Company]
[Address]
[City, State ZIP]

Dear [Mr./Ms. Last Name]:

Thanks for your inquiry regarding your potential employee, [Name]. I am sorry but it has been so long since [First Name] worked for us that I have trouble remembering the details of [his/her] employment.

I can say that I recall [he/she] got along well with [His/Her] teammates and was always eager to learn new things. [His/Her] work was always accurate and I recall [First Name] was not afraid to ask about things [he/she] didn't understand. [First Name] went through a brief phase where [he/she] had a little trouble arriving on time in the morning, but [he/she] was always careful to make up the time at the end of the day.

I hope this helps you decide whether or not to hire [Name].

Sincerely,

[Your Name]
[Your Address, if not on letterhead]

Resignation

[Date]

[Name]
[Company]
[Address]
[City, State ZIP]

Dear [Mr./Ms. Last Name]:

Please consider this letter formal notification of my resignation, effective [Date].

I have decided to pursue a consulting career and to help my [husband/wife] with [his/her] new business, [New Company Name], work that I feel would constitute a conflict of interest if I were to continue with [Company Name].

I am scheduled to go on an international sales trip the week before my end date. I am willing to do this if you think it is still appropriate for me to represent the company.

I will of course be sure to return all supplies and other [Company Name] materials by the last day of my employment. I would like to thank you again for allowing me to work from home part time.

If there is any opportunity for me to take on any of my current duties as a freelance consultant, I would appreciate having a conversation about that. If you would like me to prepare a proposal, please let me know.

I have appreciated the opportunities that [Company Name] has afforded me over the past two years and the flexibility to work from home.

Sincerely,

[Your Name]
[Your Address, if not on letterhead]

Always try to leave a company on a positive note, especially if you are going out on your own. You never know when your former employer could become a client. Also, you may decide at some point to return to that company. Burning bridges just makes no sense.

Retirement

[Date]

[Name]
[Company]
[Address]
[City, State ZIP]

Dear [Mr./Ms. Last Name]:

It is with great sadness that I announce the retirement of [Name]. [First Name] has been with [Company Name] for 30 years, a tenure not common in today's work world.

When [First Name] started with [Company Name], we were a four-person shop with 30 clients. Today, we have over 200 employees with offices on both the West and East Coasts of the United States and a representative in the UK and Europe. And [First Name] helped make all this happen!

Besides [his/her] talent in the industry and [his/her] great rapport with clients, we will miss [First Name]'s sense of humor. [He/She] could always be counted on to take a minor setback and bring us back to reality.

We invite all company employees to attend a retirement party for [First Name]. The East Coast party will be on June 12th and the West Coast party on June 18th. Many of you may not know that [Name] spent 12 years with [Company Name] in our West Coast office. We are flying [him/her] to the West Coast so [he/she] can have an opportunity to say farewell to our people there.

Again, I am sure you will all join me in wishing [First Name] a retirement full of R&R, golfing with friends, running on the beach with [his/her] dogs, and cooking those master chef meals with [his wife/her husband], [First Name].

Sincerely,

[Your Name]
[Your Address, if not on letterhead]

The retirement of a longtime employee should be treated as an important event. When managers show how much they value their employees, company morale is better and employees stay with the company longer.

Retirement (Internal Letter)

[Date]

All Employees
[Company]
[Address]
[City, State ZIP]

Dear Employees:

It is with a mixture of sadness and excitement that I announce the retirement of our sales manager, [Name]. [First Name] has been with the company [Number] years and has contributed greatly to our success.

[First Name]'s final day will be [Date]. We know you will join us in wishing [Him/Her] the best.

Sincerely,

[Your Name]
[Your Address, if not on letterhead]

Typically you might include any plans for a retirement in the announcement, but if the party is to be a surprise, you would want to send along a confidential memo to everyone but the retiree.

Retirement (External Letter)

[Date]

[Name]
[Company]
[Address]
[City, State ZIP]

Dear [Mr./Ms. Last Name]:

[Company Name] congratulates [Name] on [his/her] recent retirement after [Number] years with our firm.

[Name] was instrumental in the construction project of the new school in [Town], the project for which [he/she] was hired. The school has won design awards and the design has been used in somewhat altered forms in six other school systems in the country.

We will miss [First Name], but we know [he/she] will enjoy spending more time sailing in [his/her] boat, The Golly G.

Sincerely,

[Your Name]
[Your Address, if not on letterhead]

Retirement notices are often posted in business newspapers. But if a person has worked on a public project, such as a school, the retirement notice may be of more public interest.

Retirement (From Retiree)

[Date]

[Name]
[Company]
[Address]
[City, State ZIP]

Dear [Mr./Ms. Last Name]:

Please accept this letter as formal notice of my intention to retire, effective [Date], [Year]. My wife's medical concerns are requiring a lot more of my time now and I would like to be free to focus more on my personal life.

Working at [Law Firm Name] these past 15 years has been the best work of my career. I appreciate the firm's commitment to pro bono work and its dedication to the community. I hope I have contributed in some small way to the firm's success and helped it be able to carry on its good work.

I have also most appreciated the guidance and wise counsel of senior partner, [Name]. She always helped me think things through from a unique perspective and come up with just the perfect angle I needed for closing arguments or research or jury selection criteria.

Please let me know what steps I need to take in the retirement process.

Sincerely,

[Your Name]
[Your Address, if not on letterhead]

This letter would typically be addressed to your boss, with a copy also going to the HR department, depending on the size of the company.

New Policy (Internal Letter) 1

[Date]

[Name]
[Company]
[Address]
[City, State ZIP]

Dear Employees:

We have always been flexible about dress here at [Company Name]. However, in light of the extremes we have seen over the past few months, we are instituting a dress code. Please begin to follow the new rules, effective immediately:

- Jeans are fine, but they must be clean and free of holes (whether the holes are the result of use or design).

- Long pants are a must. No shorts, please. We are sorry about this rule, but there just seems to be no way to establish a standard for length.

- Shirts must be short- or long-sleeve. That means no tank tops or spaghetti-strap tops and nothing that allows underwear to show (either top or bottom).

- Please wear either close-toed shoes or sandals with socks or pantyhose. Although this is not technically a food-service company, we do deal with food products and it just is not appropriate for bare feet to be exposed.

- No hats are to be worn in the office.

- Please be judicious if you wear imprinted clothing. We definitely cannot allow any profanity. And please keep in mind that your colleagues and our customers may not agree with your political or religious sentiments—or appreciate your sense of humor. We trust that there will be no need to prohibit all imprinted clothing.

- We are not at this time going to impose rules on body jewelry and art. However, we do ask that you use your judgment and keep to a minimum the amount of body piercing or tattoos you expose. We appreciate that this is a matter of personal taste, but we believe that from a business standpoint it is better to err on the side of modesty and consideration for others.

Thank you for your understanding. We have tried to allow complete freedom of dress, but we have found that there are now just too many employees and too wide a range of tastes for that to make sense.

Sincerely,

[Your Name]

[Your Address, if not on letterhead]

Believe it or not, some people just don't realize that a bra strap hanging out from spaghetti straps just doesn't look professional. Try not to be too rigid: allow for some expression of personal taste, but do not apologize for making your preferences clear.

New Policy (Internal Letter) 2

[Date]

[Name]
[Company]
[Address]
[City, State ZIP]

Dear [Mr./Ms. Last Name]:

Beginning with the [Date] pay period, employees wishing to do so can add pet insurance to their benefits. Pet insurance rates vary by type of pet and age, so please refer to the enclosed information to help calculate your premium.

We know that a lot of our employees have pets and we are pleased to offer this benefit. We hope that those of you with pets will take advantage of it. Then please let us know about any use you make of it, so we can assess the value of this new benefit to our pet owners.

Sincerely,

[Your Name]
[Your Address, if not on letterhead]

Always be sure to announce any additional benefits as soon as possible.

Promotion (Internal Letter) 1

It's a tough situation when an employee dies, but when another employee replaces him or her, the new person in that position deserves recognition. It is best to keep it simple.

[Date]

[Name]
[Company]
[Address]
[City, State ZIP]

Dear [Mr./Ms. Last Name]:

I am pleased to announce that [Name] has been promoted to [Position Title]. While we all remain incredibly sad that [Name of Predecessor] passed away, I know [he/she] would be glad to know that [his/her] department will be in the able hands of [his/her] long-time assistant. [First Name] has been shepherding the department since [First Name of Predecessor] took a medical leave of absence three months ago.

I am confident this will be smooth transition and we encourage you to personally congratulate [First Name] on [his/her] promotion.

Sincerely,

[Your Name]
[Your Address, if not on letterhead]

Promotion (Internal Letter) 2

[Date]

All Employees
[Company]
[Address]
[City, State ZIP]

Dear Employees:

I am pleased to report that we have created a new position of [Title], which will be filled by [Name]. [First Name] is currently [Title] and has well earned this promotion. We expect this new position to be the beginning of a whole new category of clients and an exciting opportunity to the company. As many of you know, [First Name] worked in [Industry] before joining as at [Company Name], which makes [him/her] a logical choice for developing these clients.

Although we are still deciding the details of this new position, we know that the [Department Name] will now fall under [First Name]'s supervision. We will keep everyone apprised of developments as we continue to create a job description for [First Name].

Sincerely,

[Your Name]
[Your Address, if not on letterhead]

Although announcing a promotion before a job description is fully developed may seem a little premature, it is usually best to offset the rumor mill with truth as soon as possible. Doing that in writing is best. Send out an announcement and post copies on the company bulletin boards.

Promotion (External Letter)

This kind of announcement can also be created as a press release, especially if the company is publicly held.

[Date]

[Name]
[Company]
[Address]
[City, State ZIP]

Dear [Mr./Ms. Last Name]:

[Company Name] is pleased to announce the promotion to CFO of [Name]. [Mr./Ms. Last Name] has been an employee of [Company Name] since [Date], starting out in the accounting department. [Mr./Ms. Last Name] has been instrumental in the growth of [Company Name] in the past [number] years. [He/She] well deserves this promotion.

Sincerely,

[Your Name]
[Your Address, if not on letterhead]

Layoff (Internal Letter) 1

[Date]

[Name]
[Company]
[Address]
[City, State ZIP]

Dear [Mr./Ms. Last Name]:

The company directors have met for many hours to address a serious shortfall in revenue for this year. We have trimmed several budgets, but we have done as much trimming of budgets as we can and continue to operate safely and effectively. Unfortunately, we are forced to consolidate some positions.

The results of that consolidation is that we are losing ten positions, so we must lay off the ten people in those positions. Your position is one of those that we are losing through the consolidation.

Your last day with [Company Name] will be [Day] [Date]. We are contracting with a career counselor, who will be available to you soon. We will update you on the terms of your lay-off within the next few days.

We thank you for your [Number] years of service to [Company Name].

Sincerely,

[Your Name]
[Your Address, if not on letterhead]

Hopefully the managers of the affected employees will have told them about the layoffs in person before the employees receive this letter. Don't be too apologetic—business is ultimately business—but be sure to tell the employees as much as you can as soon as you can. Most employees deserve at least that much consideration.

Layoff (Internal Letter) 2

In a situation like this, a letter notifying employees of an impending layoff gives them a little time to think about volunteering and/or about what they will be doing if laid off, voluntarily or otherwise. Of course, the managers of the affected departments should speak with their employees immediately and the other managers should reassure their employees, also immediately.

[Date]

All Employees
[Company]
[Address]
[City, State ZIP]

Dear Employees:

We don't want to alarm everyone, but we think it's best to let you know as soon as possible that there will be a company-wide temporary layoff of [Number] workers at the end of the summer rush. Notices will be sent out the week of [Date 1] and the layoffs will take place as of [Date 2].

As all of you were warned when accepting employment at [Company Name], temporary layoffs happen annually. We are typically able to bring back the affected employees sometime between Thanksgiving and the Christmas holidays.

Managers will be speaking very soon with all departments affected by this layoff, to determine how many of these layoffs can be voluntary. We know many of you have small businesses to run or school-age children with whom you'd like to take a summer vacation; we hope that those employees and any others who are financially able will volunteer for the layoff.

Thank you all for your hard work.

Sincerely,

[Your Name]
[Your Address, if not on letterhead]

Layoffs (Internal-External)

[Date]

[Name]
[Company]
[Address]
[City, State ZIP]

Dear [Mr./Ms. Last Name]:

After a mild winter of little snow, we are sorry to have to take drastic measures and lay off some of our staff earlier than expected but it is a necessity. This layoff is effective this Monday. Final checks will be distributed at the end of the day Sunday.

We have appreciated your dedication to our ski resort, and we encourage you to check back with us for employment in October, if your circumstances allow.

Thank you for your work. We hope we can work together again next ski season.

Sincerely,

[Your Name]
[Your Address, if not on letterhead]

Don't encourage employees you're laying off to check back for employment if you are not sincere about wanting them back. It's ok if this is seen by outsiders.

## Chapter 13

Public Relations Letters and Press Releases

Free publicity is almost always more effective than paid advertising. The fact that businesses pay for advertising is indicative of the fact that there is only so much free publicity to go around.

Free publicity can result from a press release. A newspaper editor reads your release and decides the content is worthy of a story. The editor will assign a reporter to interview you and generate a news story based on your press release. Or, in many cases, a press release is printed verbatim.

Format

Press releases have a specific format that is very simple and for a reason. With a press release you are trying to get the attention of a busy editor, giving that person reason to want to print your press release or to call you for more information and possibly a full-length article on the subject of your press release or perhaps on your company in general.

Quite literally, a press release is a release of information to the press. You don't want to send out so many press releases that editors toss them into as soon as they see your name. However, there are many reasons for generating a press release, including the following:

- hiring a new employee
- offering a new product or service, just before you make it available
- winning an award (either the company or an individual employee)

Keep your press release to one page whenever possible. This is a standard format:

- Start with a headline. It should attract attention, summing up your text in six to eight words.

- Next, put the words "FOR IMMEDIATE RELEASE" or "FOR RELEASE ON [Date]" (in capital letters) to tell the editor when the press release can be made public. If the information is very time-sensitive, you should control it by submitting a press release only when the information can go public, because sometimes editors miss or disregard the release date.

- Preface the text with a dateline. Put the city and state from which the release is being generated or in which the event is taking place, followed by the date of the release.

- In the first paragraph, or even the first sentence, interest the reader with the most gripping part of your news. Don't expect the reader to go much further in your release unless you catch his or her attention immediately.

- Write the text of your press release as carefully as if it were going straight into print—because that happens sometimes. Don't expect an editor to correct or improve your writing.

- End the release with a short paragraph about your company and a brief history to provide a context for your news. Don't assume that the editor or the readers know your company. This is generally boilerplate: just insert the same paragraph into every release. If you can customize it for that particular new event, do so.

- Provide a contact to encourage inquiries from journalists. Give a name, a title, a phone number, and an e-mail address.

- If your release will be longer than one page, end the first page with "MORE." However, keep in mind that for press releases less is more—and more is usually more likely to get tossed.

- Mark the end of your release. The common way to mark the end is with a symbol—three asterisks ("* * *"), three pound signs ("# # #"), or "30" (the standard way in which journalists end their stories).

Public Relations Letters

Public relations letters are different from press releases in that the letters are typically not intended to be released to the media. Public relations letters may be between two businesses or from a business to an individual.

Often the public relations letter is seeking to clarify a point of confusion—a mistake that is made, a clarification of a property boundary with an explanation to owners of properties along that boundary, or a description of a charitable organization that a company has started or contributed to.

Companies have put public relations letters in full-page ads in large newspapers like *The New York Times* to outline a company policy or to improve the corporate image that has been damaged by a lawsuit or media coverage.

Hopefully you won't need to do any PR to improve your company's reputation or to apologize for a serious mistake. But knowing how to conduct a positive public relations campaign in print is important in any business.

Press Release: New Product 1

FOR IMMEDIATE RELEASE

DATE:

CONTACT:

POPULAR WINEMAKER ADDS NEW WINE

[CITY], [STATE]—[Company Name] is pleased to announce the company's first red wine. Called [Name of Wine], this addition of the popular Cabernet Sauvignon is sure to be a hit with wine lovers nationwide.

[Name of Wine] will be available just before the holiday season wherever wines are sold.

[Company Name] was established in [Year] and in the past [Number] years has become a premier winemaker in the Pacific Northwest. [Company Name] already offers several varieties of white wines that are shipped internationally.

For more information on the company and its complete list of wines, please visit the [Company Name] Web site at [URL]. For more information about [Name of Wine], contact [Name], media liaison, at [Phone Number] or [E-Mail Address].

* * *

Always start your press release with the name of your company. You want to be sure to make it clear right from the beginning who issued the press release.

Press Release: New Product 2

FOR IMMEDIATE RELEASE

DATE:

CONTACT:

New Product Will Be Welcomed by Plumbers

[DATELINE]—[Company Name], makers of the [Product Name(s)], are pleased to announce the addition of a new product to their already successful line. [New Product Name], developed in conjunction with NASA's shuttle program for use in space, will make every plumber's life easier with its ability to be used either hot or cold and to seal even the toughest of leaks.

To ensure that all plumbers get a chance to try our product, we are offering a free sample. Go to our Web site at [URL] and click on "free sample" or call 1-888-555-5555 to obtain your free sample. We are confident once you try [Product Name], you will be calling to place an order!

[Company Name] has been in the plumbing supply business for over 75 years. Located in [City], [State], we serve plumbers across the United States.

* * *

Always include your company's Web site address in every press release. You can keep your press release short but give readers the best source to go to get all the further information they need.

Press Release: New Service 1

FOR IMMEDIATE RELEASE

DATE:

CONTACT:

[Company Name] Adding Delivery Service

[DATELINE]—[Company Name] is excited to announce that we are now offering delivery service to job sites within a 50-mile radius of any of our stores. Out on a job site and not able to spare a worker to make a trip to the hardware store or lumber yard? We will now come to you!

Call us at 1-888-555-5555 and place your order. We will tell you when we will be there. You can pay conveniently with a credit card right on site, or we can establish accounts with appropriate credit references.

Don't waste your valuable time running around for supplies. Let us do it for you!

*   *   *

When announcing a new service, always be sure to tell potential customers what the benefits are to them.

Press Release: New Service 2

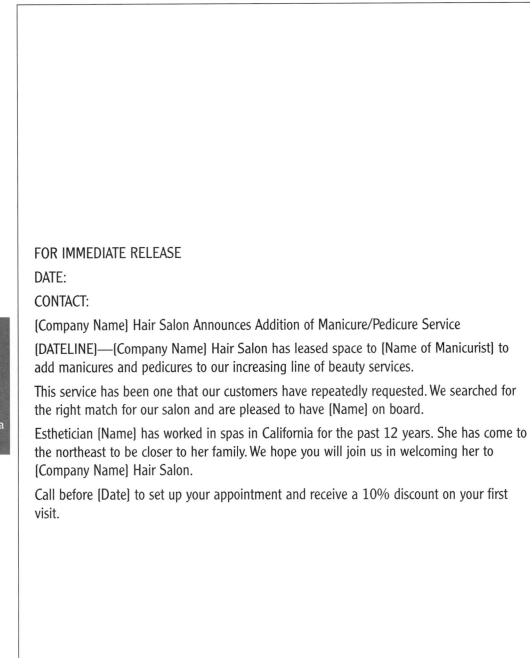

Adding a new service and promoting a new employee with special skills are always good reasons to generate a press release.

FOR IMMEDIATE RELEASE

DATE:

CONTACT:

[Company Name] Hair Salon Announces Addition of Manicure/Pedicure Service

[DATELINE]—[Company Name] Hair Salon has leased space to [Name of Manicurist] to add manicures and pedicures to our increasing line of beauty services.

This service has been one that our customers have repeatedly requested. We searched for the right match for our salon and are pleased to have [Name] on board.

Esthetician [Name] has worked in spas in California for the past 12 years. She has come to the northeast to be closer to her family. We hope you will join us in welcoming her to [Company Name] Hair Salon.

Call before [Date] to set up your appointment and receive a 10% discount on your first visit.

Press Release: Change of Ownership

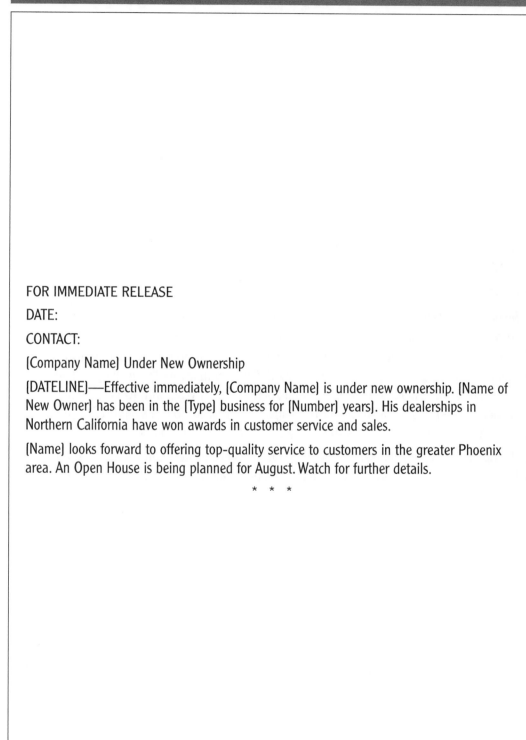

FOR IMMEDIATE RELEASE

DATE:

CONTACT:

[Company Name] Under New Ownership

[DATELINE]—Effective immediately, [Company Name] is under new ownership. [Name of New Owner] has been in the [Type] business for [Number] years]. His dealerships in Northern California have won awards in customer service and sales.

[Name] looks forward to offering top-quality service to customers in the greater Phoenix area. An Open House is being planned for August. Watch for further details.

* * *

When announcing change of ownership, never say negative things about the old business. Instead focus on the positive elements of the change, especially any awards the new owner has earned.

Press Release: New Hire 1

FOR IMMEDIATE RELEASE

DATE:

CONTACT:

Architectural Firm Hires New Architect with Commercial Experience

[DATELINE]—[Company Name] is excited to announce the expansion into commercial architectural services with the hiring of [Name]. [Name] was previously with the [Other Company Name] in Houston. [He/She] is the designer of many award-winning buildings, including several public schools. Prior to [his/her] [number] years with [Other Company Name], [Name] was the architect for buildings at the [College/University]. [HeShe] graduated from [University] with a Master's Degree in Architecture in [Date].

[Company Name] is a full-service architectural firm since [Date], with a staff of 16 architects. No project is too large or two small. [Company Name] also employs two landscape architects and several interior designers.

*   *   *

Never miss an opportunity to relate a brief history of your company so people will be comfortable calling you with their business.

Press Release: New Hire 2

FOR IMMEDIATE RELEASE

DATE:

CONTACT:

[Company Name] Hires New CEO

[DATELINE]—[Company Name] is pleased to announce the hiring of [Name], former CEO of [Former Company Name], an international firm specializing in [Industry].

[Name] will bring [Company Name] to the global market. [He/She] is formerly of [Earlier Company Name], where [he/she] was responsible for a 20% growth in sales in two years. [Name] has become known for [his/her] management style and has become a successful conference speaker.

[Name] lives in the Boston area with [his wife/her husband]. [His/Her] two children are in college. [Name] will divide [His/Her] time between Boston and New York until the company completes the move of corporate headquarters to Boston.

[Company Name] was a start-up venture five years ago and has rapidly become a key player in the U.S. market. Founder and CEO [Name] died of cancer in January.

*   *   *

New Partnership

FOR IMMEDIATE RELEASE

DATE:

CONTACT:

[Company 1 Name] Joins with [Company 2 Name] to Become Full-Service Heating and Cooling Provider

[DATELINE]—[Company 1 Name] has joined forces with [Company 2 Name] to offer the seacoast area full-service HVAC system installation and repair. [Company 1 Name] provides residential service, while [Company 2 Name] provides HVAC service to commercial accounts.

The new company will be called [Company Names Combined]. [Company 1] will move to the [Company 2] site, where there is ample office and warehouse space. The relocation will be completed by September 30, just in time for the busy heating season.

No employees will be laid off. [Company 1 Name] founder and CEO, [Name], will retire, effective September 1. [Name], CEO of [Company 2 Name], will head up the new company. Other management changes will be announced as they are decided.

[Company 1 Name] was established in 1962, serving residents of the eight-town seacoast area. The company has been family-run since its founding. [Company 2 Name] has been a commercial provider of HVAC service to northern New England since 1935.

* * *

Press Release: Damage Control 1

FOR IMMEDIATE RELEASE

DATE:

CONTACT:

[RESTAURANT NAME] HIRES FIRM TO DO ANTISEPTIC CLEANING

[DATELINE]—[Restaurant Name] hired [Cleaning Firm Name] to perform a thorough antiseptic cleaning of the restaurant following a highly publicized food poisoning incident. Although there is no solid evidence proving that the death of [Name] was directly related to eating at [Restaurant Name], the popular establishment voluntarily ordered a thorough cleaning of the entire restaurant, kitchen, dining rooms, and bathrooms, which was completed on Monday May 11.

[Restaurant Name] is now open for business and looks forward to continuing its 30-year history of great food at great prices.

*   *   *

Negative publicity needs a direct response. A press release telling about action taken to solve the source of the negative publicity can go a long way to re-affirming customers' faith and loyalty. In cases like this, however, care needs to be taken to avoid even the appearance of admission of guilt as there is likely a lawsuit involved. Always have a lawyer look over this kind of press release before releasing it.

Press Release: Damage Control 2

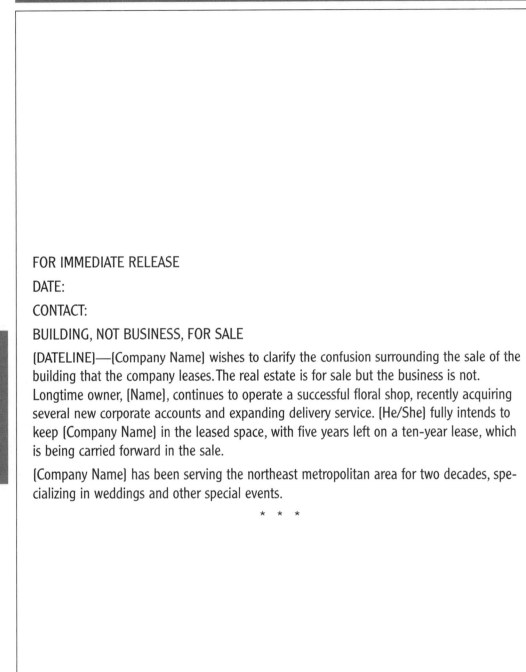

FOR IMMEDIATE RELEASE

DATE:

CONTACT:

BUILDING, NOT BUSINESS, FOR SALE

[DATELINE]—[Company Name] wishes to clarify the confusion surrounding the sale of the building that the company leases. The real estate is for sale but the business is not. Longtime owner, [Name], continues to operate a successful floral shop, recently acquiring several new corporate accounts and expanding delivery service. [He/She] fully intends to keep [Company Name] in the leased space, with five years left on a ten-year lease, which is being carried forward in the sale.

[Company Name] has been serving the northeast metropolitan area for two decades, specializing in weddings and other special events.

*   *   *

Press releases can help clarify confusion by triggering papers to go find out the real story, especially if the release goes out during a slow news season.

Press Release: Joint Venture—New Service

FOR IMMEDIATE RELEASE

DATE:

CONTACT:

TWO SUCCESSFUL COMPANIES JOIN FORCES

[DATELINE]—[Company 1 Name], maker of organic coffee, and [Company 2 Name], small airline serving the mid-Atlantic region, have joined forces to offer [Company 1 Name] coffee on all flights. [Company 1 Name] is a subscription-based coffee company and will include subscription cards in the seat pockets of the airline. Customers who enjoy [Company 1 Name]'s fresh organic coffee on board can easily fill out the subscription form and begin enjoying [Company 1 Name] coffee at home. A free coffeemaker is provided with each new subscription.

[Company 1 Name], based in [Town Name], has been in the organic coffee business for ten years. [Company 2 Name] is a new airline started this year to fill the need for short flights to serve the mid-Atlantic region.

When announcing a joint venture, you should name both companies, but don't hesitate to mention your own company several times. The other company will do the same for itself with the press releases it generates.

Press Release: Award Announcement

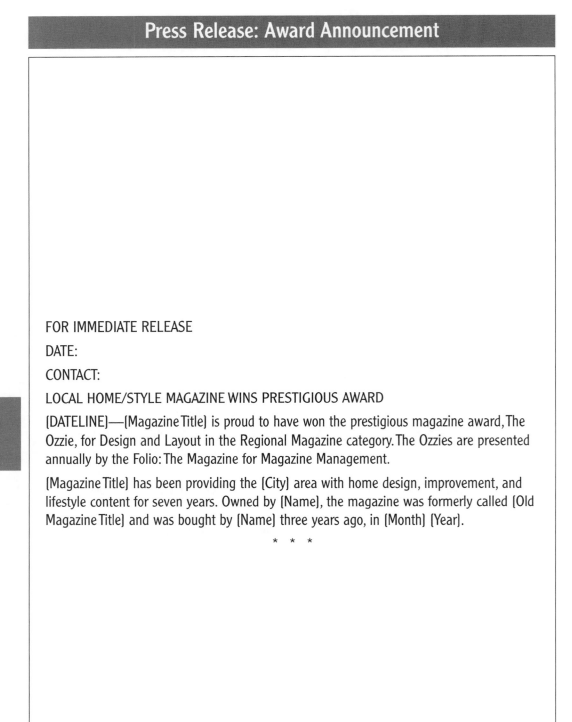

FOR IMMEDIATE RELEASE

DATE:

CONTACT:

LOCAL HOME/STYLE MAGAZINE WINS PRESTIGIOUS AWARD

[DATELINE]—[Magazine Title] is proud to have won the prestigious magazine award, The Ozzie, for Design and Layout in the Regional Magazine category. The Ozzies are presented annually by the Folio: The Magazine for Magazine Management.

[Magazine Title] has been providing the [City] area with home design, improvement, and lifestyle content for seven years. Owned by [Name], the magazine was formerly called [Old Magazine Title] and was bought by [Name] three years ago, in [Month] [Year].

* * *

Never let any award slip by without a press release.

Press Release: Move/Building Purchase

FOR IMMEDIATE RELEASE

DATE:

CONTACT:

[Company Name] MOVES TO NEW BUILDING

[DATELINE]—[Company Name] has purchased a warehouse on [Name of Road] in suburban [City] and will move its entire book-publishing operation there by late August. The warehouse is 60 percent larger than the company's current warehouse and includes a wing of offices spaces, allowing the entire company—from editorial to distribution—to be housed under one roof.

[Company Name] has been in the book publishing business for 26 years. During that time it has grown from publishing ten books a year to publishing 150 books a year and distributing books for several other publishers, including the popular [Name of Series] travel guides.

*   *   *

Use a press release to announce a building purchase and move. Send it to your customer list as well as newspapers and magazines to be sure all of your customers are alerted to your

Press Release: Opening New Branch

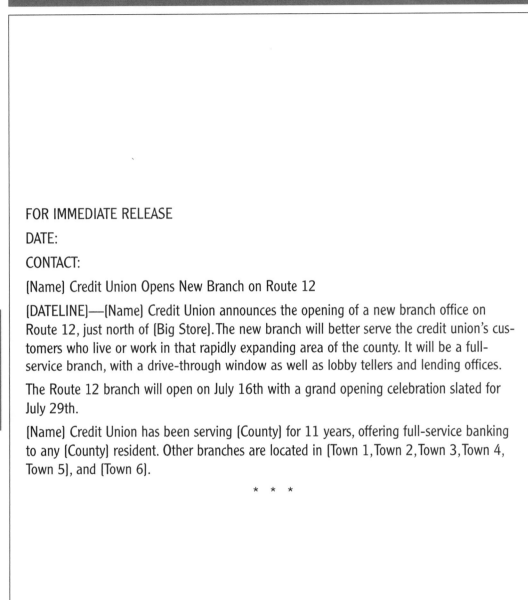

FOR IMMEDIATE RELEASE

DATE:

CONTACT:

[Name] Credit Union Opens New Branch on Route 12

[DATELINE]—[Name] Credit Union announces the opening of a new branch office on Route 12, just north of [Big Store]. The new branch will better serve the credit union's customers who live or work in that rapidly expanding area of the county. It will be a full-service branch, with a drive-through window as well as lobby tellers and lending offices.

The Route 12 branch will open on July 16th with a grand opening celebration slated for July 29th.

[Name] Credit Union has been serving [County] for 11 years, offering full-service banking to any [County] resident. Other branches are located in [Town 1, Town 2, Town 3, Town 4, Town 5], and [Town 6].

*   *   *

A new branch office deserves a press release. Be sure to include in your announcement any plans for a grand opening.

Press Release: Expansion to New Market

FOR IMMEDIATE RELEASE

DATE:

CONTACT:

[Company Name] Now Serving Lakes Region

[DATELINE]—[Company Name] has hired a new sales representative to open up new territory in the Lakes Region of [State]. [Name] has 15 years' experience selling pet foods and related products and knows our brand and our industry well. Accounts can rely on [him/her] to provide accurate information and help them keep their shelves stocked with the best products for their market.

[Name] lives in [Town] with [his wife/her husband] and three cats and a dog. [He/She] is a licensed veterinary technician and has been showing dogs in agility and obedience for ten years.

[Name] will be calling accounts to set up appointments soon. [He/She] can be reached at 555-555-5555 and will maintain an office at [Company Name] headquarters at [Address].

[Company Name] has been in the business of providing quality natural pet foods for 12 years. Our foods can be found in most stores that sell quality pet foods.

*   *   *

Although good sales reps pretty quickly discover all the potential customers in their market, always give contact information so that those customers anxious to meet with the rep can schedule an appointment as soon as possible.

Press Release: Annual Shareholders' Meeting

Publicly held companies are required to hold and announce shareholders' meetings. Most public companies have a shareholder liaison whose specific job is to handle questions from shareholders. This person should always be named with contact information in any press releases about company stock and financial

FOR IMMEDIATE RELEASE

DATE:

CONTACT:

[Company Name] Announces Annual Shareholders' Meeting

[DATELINE]—[Company Name], [Address], will be holding its annual shareholders' meeting on March 17th at 2pm in the Grand Ballroom of the [Hotel Name]. The following business will be conducted at the meeting:

1) The release of financial statements for the year ending 31 December 2010;

2) The election of replacements for directors whose terms are ending;

3) Any other business matters that are added to the agenda before the meeting.

*   *   *

Letter to Shareholders

[Date]

Dear [Company Name] Shareholder:

Enclosed is important information regarding your account. The 2008 tax law reforms brought important legal changes in the areas of capital gains and dividend distributions.

Please take a few minutes to read the highlights of these changes outlined on the next page. Enclosed you will find updated documents, which you should be sure to read to fully understand these changes. We have also enclosed a Change of Beneficiary form so you can update your beneficiary information if you wish.

For more information, please contact us at [Phone Number] ([Days, Hours]).

To review a copy of IRS Publication [Number], look online at www.irs.gov or call [Phone Number].

We thank you for your confidence in [Name of Company].

Sincerely,

[Name]
[Title]

Press Release: Retirement of Sales Manager

FOR IMMEDIATE RELEASE

DATE:

CONTACT:

AWARD-WINNING SALES MANAGER RETIRES AFTER [number] YEARS

[DATELINE]—[Name], Sales Manager at [Company Name] is retiring effective June 16th. [Name] has been with [Company Name] for [number] years. [Name] started as a picker and packer in the warehouse and [his/her] work ethic and dedication brought [him/her] up through the ranks to sales. [He/She] has been Sales Manager for the past 20 years, with a remarkable increase in revenue every year [he/she] has been in that position.

[Name] has won numerous awards, both within the company and within the appliance industry, including a car and a trip to Hawaii. [Name] coached Little League when [hjis/her] oldest [son/daughter] joined the team, bringing the [Team Name] to the state championships on several occasions.

[Name] will begin [his/her] retirement relaxing on Lake Jones with [His Wife/Her Husband] and their Chris-Craft boat, which they restored themselves. Golf, reading, traveling, and continuing volunteer work at the local food pantry are also in [his/her] plans.

*   *   *

This press release should be directed toward the business pages of newspapers and any specific business newspapers in your region. They are always on the lookout for "people in the news" stories.

Press Release: Merger

FOR IMMEDIATE RELEASE

DATE:

CONTACT:

ATTORNEYS MERGER

[DATELINE]—Smith Law Office is pleased to announce that my associate, [Name], and I have joined the law firm of Jones, Jones, & Edwards. The new firm will be known as Jones, Jones, Smith, & Edwards. We have relocated Smith Law Office to the Jones, Jones, & Edwards location at [Address]. We can still be reached through our former phone number, [Phone Number].

Combining our practices allows Jones, Jones, Smith, & Edwards to offer a complete range of service in all legal areas, including business start-up and general corporate practice, real estate, residential and commercial lending, personal injury, bankruptcy, divorce, and other domestic matters.

This merger will create a full service practice to the people of the greater metro area. Smith Law Office has been in practice for over 20 years. Together with Jones, Jones, & Edwards, we offer a combined 85 years of practice in legal matters in the tri-state area.

*   *   *

You will send individual letters to your clients outlining the details of the merger, where their files will be, and what they need to do to continue or terminate the relationship. You can cull the appropriate information from that letter to create a press release, allowing you to not have to create two pieces of written information from scratch.

Press Release: Sale of Business

You could say something like "the current owner will not stay on to help with the transition" but that sounds too negative—remember, the press release is being generated by you, and needs to impart the message and tone you wish the world to hear when they hear about your company.

FOR IMMEDIATE RELEASE

DATE:

CONTACT:

[Name] PURCHASES [Company Name]

[DATELINE]—[Name] has purchased [Company Name]. The deal was finalized on Friday May 12th. Transfer of ownership is immediate.

All current employees will be remaining with [Company Name], which has been a premier shirtmaker for 35 years. [Name] owns several other garment companies. [He/She] has been in the textile industry for over 40 years, starting out in the warehouse of a New York fabric importer and working [his/her] way up to CEO of a multimillion-dollar garment maker in New Jersey.

[Company Name] has suffered financially over the last six years. This transfer of ownership will allow economies of scale that are expected to enable the company to turn around and get back into the black, which is projected to happen within two years.

*   *   *

Press Release: Conference Presentation

FOR IMMEDIATE RELEASE

DATE:

CONTACT:

CEO OF LOCAL COMPANY ASKED TO PRESENT AT NATIONAL CONFERENCE

[DATELINE]—[Name], CEO of [Company Name] has been asked to present at the upcoming national conference for the Association of Residential Home Builders. As owner of the premier vinyl siding company in the country, he will speak on the advantages of vinyl over wood siding and the advances in the industry over the past 25 years.

The conference is to be held in Dallas from April 8th to the 12th, 2009.

[Company Name] is an international vinyl siding manufacturer established in 1980. [Name] has been with the company since its inception and has been CEO for the last 15 years.

*   *   *

Being asked to present at a conference indicates that the person is well respected in his field and is worth being announced through a press release.

Letter to Editor: Reacting to News Story

Letters to the editor can serve a similar purpose to a press release. Be sure to keep your letter as a clarification, not sour grapes, to give it the best chance of being published.

[Date]

[Newspaper Name]

[Address]

Dear Editor,

The article in Friday's edition of [name of newspaper] regarding the variance request by my company had some inaccuracies that need to be clarified.

First, we did not start building despite the wetlands zoning. The building in that area had been permitted, but a concern was brought before the zoning board of appeals and we had to stop building to await the outcome of the appeal. We are happy to say that the appeal was not granted and we have begun to move forward once again with our construction.

Second, the wetlands is not home to endangered species. There are no endangered species listed in the wildlife inventory for that wetland.

All of this said, I would like to emphasize that [Name of Company] takes its responsibility to the environment seriously. We have worked hard to impact the wetlands as minimally as possible while still being able to use our property to the best advantage for our company.

Sincerely,

[Name]

[Title]

[Address]

*   *   *

Press Release: Announce Award of Bid

FOR IMMEDIATE RELEASE

DATE:

CONTACT:

[Company Name] HIRED FOR STATE FLOOD CLEANUP

[DATELINE]—[Company Name] won the bid from the state of [State] for flood cleanup and repair of damaged roads. Hundreds of miles of state roads are in need of ditch and drainage repair after two weeks of often torrential rain in May.

Work will begin immediately in the hardest hit eastern part of the state and fan out across the rest of the state. All roads will be repaired by the Labor Day weekend.

[Company Name] is an excavating and paving firm established in 1966. Located in [Town], [State], the firm is run by the second generation of [Family Name], having been started by [Name]. [Company Name] is a full-service excavating and paving service that does both residential and commercial work.

*   *   *

Winning a bid proposal provides a great opportunity to toot your own horn! Bids are not always awarded based on low price—your business must have proven to do good work as well. These are the kinds of things that will stick in the minds of potential customers who read this press release.

Press Release: New Feature

Any time your business offers a new feature, promote it with a short press release. In a case like this, be sure to emphasize safety prominently in the release.

FOR IMMEDIATE RELEASE

DATE:

CONTACT:

[HEADLINE]

[DATELINE]—Water World is ready to open Memorial Weekend with four new water rides, including a state-of-the-art jet surge, the only ride of its kind in the country. All four new rides have the highest safety ratings for amusement park water rides.

These new rides add to the fun that Water World water park provides for kids of all ages.

Water World has been open since 1995 and is the premier water park in the Upper Midwest.

* * *

## Chapter 14

Letters to Government and Regulatory Agencies

Businesses operate under bureaucratic regulations on many levels—town, state, federal. You may need to write a letter to request a zoning change or to explain a request on a permit application. Lots of work for state and federal government requires submission of bids and proposals and letters accompanying each.

Much of the need for dealing with government and regulatory agencies will depend on the business you are in—dry cleaning, pest and lawn care services, contracting, and automobile-related businesses will have several layers of regulations to dig through, especially if you do hazardous waste removal or need to dispose of used oil. Any use of radioactive materials will require much back-and-forth correspondence to sort through the regulatory process.

Most businesses will at least be dealing with signage, trash removal, and perhaps some variance requests to zoning regulations.

Although the letters accompanying these forms and requests usually don't need to be long—the forms themselves often cover the minute details—they do need to contain pertinent information to get your request submitted expeditiously and to make sure you don't miss critical deadlines.

Seeking Information

[Date]

[Name]
[Address]
[City, State ZIP]

Dear [Mr./Ms. Last Name]:

I am considering adding nuclear imaging to my veterinary practice. I am looking for information on obtaining licensing for nuclear medicine and the regulations controlling it after licensing has been obtained.

I would appreciate any information you could provide at this early stage in my plan.

Sincerely,

[Your Name]
[Your Address, if not on letterhead]

This could be directed to OSHA, who may have the information or certainly can direct you to the right place—and with nuclear/radioactive materials, there may be several "right places" you need to be in touch with.

Seeking RFP Details

[Date]

[Name]
[Address]
[City, State ZIP]

Dear [Mr./Ms. Last Name]:

I read the notice for your of an RFP for the [job title] for the city of [City/State] in the [Newspaper].

Please send the complete RFP as soon as possible so I can complete my proposal in time to meet your deadline.

Thank you.

Sincerely,

[Your Name]
[Your Address, if not on letterhead]

Most RFPs are now available on the Internet. If the ad doesn't indicate it is, you will want to send a letter, but be timely about it as the deadlines for sending proposals are usually inflexible.

Government RFP Proposal Cover Letter

[Date]

[Name]
[Address]
[City, State ZIP]

Dear [Mr./Ms. Last Name]:

Enclosed please find my proposal per your RFP for the [name of job] posted in [Name of Newspaper] on [date].

My proposal is broken down to match the six parts of your RFP and covers all the relevant points outlined in the RFP.

I am confident our firm could provide the city of [City Name] with the high level of services you are seeking. I am happy to be available to answer any questions that might arise as you make your decision.

I look forward to hearing from you.

Sincerely,

[Your Name]
[Your Address, if not on letterhead]

The proposal in response to an RFP should speak for itself, but always include a brief cover letter. The letter is mostly cursory, but should point out any unusual elements in your proposal.

Letter Requesting Variance

[Date]

[Name]
[Address]
(City, State ZIP]

Dear [Mr./Ms. Last Name]:

I have a small business operating out of my home, which currently falls under the regulations appropriate for the rural residential zoning in my area. My business space needs have outgrown my ability to house my business in my primary residence.

I would like to convert an outbuilding to my business office. The regulations for home businesses in rural residential zoning, as I understand them, require that the home business be operated in the primary residence. Therefore, I am requesting a variance to this regulation.

Attached you will find a to-scale drawing of my property that shows the residence and the outbuilding in which I am proposing to set up my office. As this drawing shows, the use of this outbuilding as an office has no additional impact on the neighborhood. My business as a freelance writer requires little in the way of traffic to my house, with the exception of courier vehicles making on average of two deliveries per week.

I am happy to answer any further questions and look forward to your response.

Sincerely,

[Your Name]
[Your Address, if not on letterhead]

This letter is directed to a town's Zoning Board of Appeals, which typically results in a public hearing so that any abuttors to the property will get the chance to express their concerns and understand the request better. Any accompanying enclosures you can provide that further explain the request can be very helpful to ensuring that the board fully understands your request.

Letter Requesting Environmental Permit

[Date]

[Name]
[Address]
[City, State ZIP]

Dear [Mr./Ms. Last Name]:

I am requesting permission to fill in a small portion of wetland on a recently acquired property where I am building a small office building. This portion of wetland is dry most of the year with it actually being "wet" only during the early spring or significantly rainy spells.

As you can see from the enclosed drawing, the building itself does not impact the wetland, but the driveway planned to surround the building does. The overall drawing and inset shows the landscaping I plan to do to help minimize erosion and further damage to the wetland once the building and driveway is in place.

In compensation for this encroachment, I am offering to put the rest of the wetland in a conservation easement, with the stewardship to be determined with the help of the [Name of Town]'s conservation commission.

Sincerely,

[Your Name]
[Your Address, if not on letterhead]

Especially when a variance request has environmental impact, it is always helpful to be prepared to offer something in return like, in this case, the conservation easement on the rest of the impacted wetland.

Letter Asking to Be Put on Agenda

[Date]

[Name]
[Address]
[City, State ZIP]

Dear [Mr./Ms. Last Name]:

I am requesting to meet with the planning board as soon as there is an opening in your agenda to discuss my proposed development on [Road Name]. I have enclosed preliminary plans per my discussion with you last month.

You will note that I have moved the driveway as we discussed, as well as configured entries so that each of the three driveways accommodates several houses, therefore cutting down on the number of openings to the road, per your recommendation.

My designer and builder will also be at the meeting so we should be able to answer any questions planning board members have.

Sincerely,

[Your Name]
[Your Address, if not on letterhead]

This letter should be addressed to the Planning Board Chair. Call your town's clerk to find out that person's name and to get some sense of when the planning board meets in order to get your letter to them in a timely manner. In all likelihood, you will have had a couple conversations with this person to determine some zoning details that would have an impact on your plans.

Letter to Planning Board

You could probably do this as a phone call, but keep in mind that zoning and planning board members are often volunteer staff who have full time jobs. So anything you can do to help them be more efficient can help you get a better response— a letter outlining your questions gives them a chance to research the answers. Then when you follow up with a phone call, they have the right answers for you.

[Date]

[Name]
[Address]
[City, State ZIP]

Dear [Mr./Ms. Last Name]:

I am in the process of designing a three-unit small business office development on [Name of Road] and have a few questions that I need answered before I get much further.

1) I have heard the setbacks have changed. Is this true? If so, what are the new setback regulations?

2) Are there height limitations in that area, which I understand is in Zone 3?

3) Does the city have separate handicapped access laws or do I need to simply abide by the federal regulations?

4) Lastly, I am enclosing a rough drawing of the proposed building. Does anything jump out at you as needing change?

I appreciate your time and will follow up with a phone call in around a week to see if you have the answers to these questions.

Sincerely,

[Your Name]
[Your Address, if not on letterhead]

Letter to Zoning Board of Adjustments

[Date]

[Name]
[Address]
[City, State ZIP]

Dear [Mr./Ms. Last Name]:

I have heard through the grapevine that the town of [Name of Town] recently instituted a moratorium on building. Having bought a piece of property in town six months ago, this news concerns me. I have been designing a spec home and was hoping to begin building in two months' time.

If this is true, is there a way I can get a variance to build, considering I bought this property before the moratorium went into effect?

I called the town office but the clerk suggested I contact you directly for the answer to this question. She said you may be hard to reach, so I decided to write you a letter and am hoping you will call me with the answer as soon as possible. My number is [Phone Number].

Sincerely,

[Your Name]
[Your Address, if not on letterhead]

Planning boards and zoning boards are accustomed to getting calls from irate individuals about information they heard word-of-mouth that is often incorrect. To get a polite but direct letter requesting accurate information will be a pleasant surprise to them and will get you the information you need in a timely manner.

Letter About Signage Regulations

[Date]

[Name]
[Address]
[City, State ZIP]

Dear [Mr./Ms. Last Name]:

I am opening a coffee shop in the downtown retail area. I am submitted the attached design of my sign with full dimensions and hope everything meets signage regulations for the downtown retail district. The drawing is to scale and shows all the measurements of the sign I am planning to use.

This will be the only sign on the building so I have used what I understand to be the entire signage allotment for that area.

Sincerely,

[Your Name]
[Your Address, if not on letterhead]

Don't forget that signage usually requires a permit and is held under certain regulations. Be sure to submit your plans before you spend any money getting the sign made.

Seeking Information

[Date]

[Name]
[Address]
[City, State ZIP]

Dear [Mr./Ms. Last Name]:

I am considering purchasing property in [Name of Town] but I am self-employed and need to know the regulations about home-based businesses in [Town].

My business is as a licensed massage therapist. I would have clients coming to my home, on average of five a day. I carry liability insurance over and above my homeowner's policy. Ideally, I would plan to find a piece of property that either has a separate building that I could renovate for my business or enough space to build one.

Thank you in advance for your information.

Sincerely,

[Your Name]
[Your Address, if not on letterhead]

This letter would be directed to the chair of the town's planning board. The planning board is typically the keeper of such information. Don't expect there to be a pamphlet, however, to answer your questions. You will probably end up speaking to someone personally—and they often want you to already have a property in mind so they can speak specifically to that property. Your real estate agent should also be able to help you in this kind of matter, but keep in mind their priority is selling real estate, not being familiar with every little town regulation. It's best to go directly to the source.

## Chapter 15

Social Protocol

Following good business etiquette is key to helping you stand out from the crowd. In this email age, you can get by with a quick email congratulating someone on a promotion or landing a huge account or expressing condolences on the loss of a colleague or family member. But the good old-fashioned congratulations or sympathy letter is still very much in vogue and recommended in many circumstances. Creating thank-you letters and welcome letters and apology letters is a fine art worth learning and using.

While you are promoting good PR with these kinds of letters, you are also getting one more opportunity to get your name in front of people with whom you do or want to do business. Of course, this is not the only reason to send letters of this kind—you also want to be genuine in your sympathy or congratulations! But people who send these letters are remembered.

Sympathy Letters

For something as personal as sympathy, look for a blank card that has a peaceful image on it and buy a dozen to keep in the office. You can hand-write your letter in the card and personalize it whenever possible. Sympathy messages are difficult for most people to write, but put a little thought behind it and you will be amazed at the response from recipients.

Thank-You Letters

Writing thank-you notes and letters is simply a must when it comes to good business etiquette. Send them any time someone goes above and beyond the call of duty—after you visit a business colleague's place of work, get a tour of your vendor's printing plant, get treated to lunch, or someone you work with puts in extra long hours to finish a major project on time. People who work for you can put thank-you letters in their employment file to prove their value as employees.

Congratulations

Lots of reasons exist to send a letter of congratulations, both personal and professional: someone gets an award, wins a bid, has a baby, gets married, or completes a degree. Recognizing the achievements of the people around you is a very simple way of getting the message across that you notice things beyond your own desk.

Introduction

Sending a letter can be a great way to introduce yourself. Perhaps you are going to visit a colleague in a foreign country, or even in your own country. A letter gives the recipient a chance to know a little more about you before you arrive. Focus on your professional life with just a little personal background.

Welcome Letters

Welcome letters can be a nice way to make a new colleague feel comfortable. Perhaps you have a new member of the management team starting in a month. Getting a letter from another manager before the new person starts breaks the ice before the new employee's first day and makes her feel like she is wanted, that the company is preparing for her arrival. Welcome letters to new businesses in your area are also a good way to begin potential B2B relationships—and include a coupon if that is applicable to your business!

Letters of Apology

You have to admit it—everyone makes mistakes. The best way to 'fess up and move on is to write a letter of apology and clear the air. An error filling a customer's order, forgetting a lunch meeting, losing or breaking something you borrowed—all of these are candidates for an apology letter.

Letters Requesting Permission

Perhaps your group would like to do a team-building hike on private property. Or you wish to use someone's photograph in your brochure.

Letter of Congratulations 1

[Date]

[Name]
[Address]
[City, State ZIP]

Dear [Mr./Ms. Last Name]:

I read in yesterday's [Newspaper Title] that your company won the prestigious [Award Name]. I am sure everyone there worked very hard to earn such an achievement. On behalf of everyone here at [Company Name], we extend a hearty congratulations!

Sincerely,

[Your Name]
[Your Address, if not on letterhead]

No need to go on and on, in most social protocol letters, it truly is "the thought that counts."

Letter of Congratulations 2

[Date]

[Name]
[Address]
[City, State ZIP]

Dear [Mr./Ms. Last Name]:

I understand from [source] that you have been promoted to [name of new position].

Congratulations!

We have always enjoyed working with you and look forward to working with you in your new capacity.

The next time I am visiting [name of company], I will be sure to call ahead and see if we can schedule a congratulatory lunch.

Sincerely,

[Your Name]
[Your Address, if not on letterhead]

Recognizing someone's personal achievement only helps solidify already strong relationships. People work very hard for promotions and appreciate acknowledgment of their success.

Letter of Introduction 1

[Date]

[Name]
[Address]
[City, State ZIP]

Dear [Mr./Ms. Last Name]:

I am writing to introduce myself as the new manager of your account with [Company Name]. Your former account manager, [Name], has moved on to another company.

I have been in the [Industry] industry for over 16 years and have always known your company to be a key player. I look forward to helping you in your continued success using our products.

My schedule brings me to [Town] on July 12th. I was hoping we could schedule a meeting over lunch that day. If that is convenient for you, please call me at [phone number] or email me at [email address].

Sincerely,

[Your Name]
[Your Address, if not on letterhead]

Although you can exchange bits of personal information over lunch, keep your letters focused on what you can do for the company, not on you.

Letter of Introduction 2

[Date]

[Name]
[Address]
[City, State ZIP]

Dear [Mr./Ms. Last Name]:

I am writing to introduce my new marketing company, [Company Name]. [Company Name] is focused around helping small businesses like yours get your name out in front of potential customers at limited cost.

We have tapped into sources of items such as key chains, calendars, and pens that can be imprinted with your name and logo for pennies-per-unit less than our competitors. And you can order in quantities as low as 50 and still get a great price.

[Company Name] is just a phone call away. Please consider calling before you are scheduled to attend a conference, trade show, or other business meeting. Don't let another opportunity slip by where you can leave people with a concrete reminder of your company.

Sincerely,

[Your Name]
[Your Address, if not on letterhead]

Always focus your sales-related letters on the benefits to the customer.

Welcome Letter 1

A new employee always appreciates feeling like the company they are going to work for is fully aware of their impending first day and has told the rest of the company too. And especially for a management team, starting right off welcoming a new manager can make a huge leap in the team relationship right from day one.

[Date]

[Name]
[Address]
[City, State ZIP]

Dear [Mr./Ms. Last Name]:

I was pleased to hear that [name of company] offered you the new manager position and that you accepted. Welcome aboard!

Your interview was the most relaxed and interesting that we conducted. I think you will be a great addition to the management team and I am very much looking forward to working with you. Your background seems to mesh well with our goals and you seem to have some unique ideas for challenging the company to achieve an even greater success than we already have.

Please feel free to call before your start date if you have any questions I can help with. I have lived in this area my entire life and can help direct you to things like a great mechanic, a reliable real estate agent, good school systems, etc.

Again, congratulations and best of luck with your move.

Sincerely,

[Your Name]
[Your Address, if not on letterhead]

Welcome Letter 2

[Date]

[Name]
[Address]
[City, State ZIP]

Dear [Mr./Ms. Last Name]:

Welcome to the [Street Name] retail neighborhood! Your homemade chocolate shop is just the kind of business that is making this street become known as the street in [name of town] on which to shop for specialty foods.

[Shop Name] has been on [Street Name] for nine years. We have seen our business grow from a mainly tourist summer clientele to a year-round customer base. I am sure you will thrive here.

As a welcome gift, I am enclosing a few coupons for a free cup of coffee and a discount card for any purchases here at [Shop Name] for you or your employees.

Again, welcome to [Street Name]. We look forward to having you!

Sincerely,

[Your Name]
[Your Address, if not on letterhead]

Small retail shop owners work so hard and usually have just a couple, if any, employees, so it is especially nice to project a "block" community in welcoming a new business to the neighborhood.

Invitation 1

[Date]

[Name]
[Address]
[City, State ZIP]

Dear [Mr./Ms. Last Name]:

[Company Name] is sponsoring the next [Town] Chamber of Commerce business-after-hours meeting on October 17th at 6pm. The meetings are held in the Chamber lobby at [Address].

Complimentary hors d'oeuvres, wine, and beer will be served. [Company Name] president will speak briefly at 7:00 pm on the subject of customer retention.

We would very much like to see you there!

Sincerely,

[Your Name]
[Your Address, if not on letterhead]

If you are going to spend money on something like a Chamber of Commerce gathering, you might as well help make sure people come! Be sure to send out invitations to your mailing list of local clients.

Invitation 2

[Date]

[Name]
[Address]
[City, State ZIP]

Dear [Mr./Ms. Last Name]:

A couple of us retailers on [Street Name] were chatting the other day and thought it might be fun and useful to initiate an annual Sidewalk Sale. We are polling our neighboring retailers to see if there is interest in this idea.

We were thinking a one-day sale with some low-key entertainment and good bargains on quality merchandise. Would you be interested in joining us in such a venture?

Please call either me at [Phone Number] or [Name] of [Company Name] at [Phone Number] to let us know of your interest.

Thanks!

Sincerely,

[Your Name]
[Your Address, if not on letterhead]

Small retailers banding together to create a retail event that none of them could generate on their own is a great community-creating thing to do. Get creative, start talking with other retailers, and spread the word with a letter of invitation to other retailers.

Letter of Apology 1

Despite our best attempts, mistakes happen. Own up to them and give some form of recompense. How much depends on how big of an impact the mistake had on the final product. Of course in most cases you will offer to redo the job, but sometimes that is not necessary.

[Date]

[Name]
[Address]
[City, State ZIP]

Dear [Mr./Ms. Last Name]:

Please accept our sincere apologies for using the wrong end papers for your recent print job, [Book Title]. I have no excuse, it was just a miscommunication.

Although I understand and appreciate that you are satisfied with the product anyway, we are committed to quality printing and giving our customers what they ask for. With that in mind, I have deducted the cost of the endpapers from your bill.

When a reprint comes due—which I am sure it will, this is a great book—please let us know if you would like to continue with the same endpapers or print the next printing with your original choice.

Again, I do apologize for the mistake. We appreciate your business and look forward to a continued relationship.

Sincerely,

[Your Name]
[Your Address, if not on letterhead]

Letter of Apology 2

[Date]

[Name]
[Address]
[City, State ZIP]

Dear [Mr./Ms. Last Name]:

I do apologize that your shipment went to the wrong address. We pride ourselves in triple checking shipment addresses, and in this case something apparently got mixed up at the custom agent's office.

As you know, we located the shipment and it is on its way to you now. I will call on Monday the 6th to be sure it arrived.

Again, please accept our sincere apologies. This is a rare mistake for us in our twenty-two years in the shipping business and I am sorry it had to happen to you. I hope you give us the opportunity in the future to prove ourselves to you.

Sincerely,

[Your Name]
[Your Address, if not on letterhead]

You will have already apologized over the phone, probably more than once! Apologies don't change what happened. And if your mistake lost your customer business, it is doubtful they will try you again. But if you don't send a formal letter of apology, they definitely will not! Always end an apology letter inviting the customer to try you again—these little things can help change their mind, and sometimes you just have to ask.

Sympathy Letter 1

Sympathy letters are difficult to write. Keep them simple, but if you knew the person, it is always nice to mention something personal.

[Date]

[Name]
[Address]
[City, State ZIP]

Dear [Mr./Ms. Last Name]:

I am so sorry to hear of the death of [Name]. It must be very hard to lose a young colleague.

I remember [Name] as such a dedicated person. I was always impressed by how many diverse interests [He/She] had outside [His/Her] career—[Name] juggled many balls and seemed to be able to keep them all in the air!

[He/She] will be greatly missed.

Most sincerely,

[Your Name]
[Your Address, if not on letterhead]

Sympathy Letter 2

[Date]

[Name]
[Address]
[City, State ZIP]

Dear [Mr./Ms. Last Name]:

I am so sorry to hear of the death of your mother. Although I never met her, from the stories you have told about her over the years I've known you, she is someone I would very much have enjoyed.

Please accept my deepest sympathy at this difficult time.

Sincerely,

[Your Name]
[Your Address, if not on letterhead]

Address a letter like this to the name of the bereaved person "and Family." Keep it short and simple. And consider writing it into a card instead of a typed letter.

Thank-You Letter for Visit

[Date]

[Name]
[Address]
[City, State ZIP]

Dear [Mr./Ms. Last Name]:

My colleagues and I had a great trip to [City] but the highlight was definitely the tour of your facility. Thank you very much for taking the time to show us around your warehouse—it is without doubt the most efficient warehouse I have ever been in. Please also thank all of your colleagues for their warm hospitality.

We also very much enjoyed dinner at the dockside lobster restaurant. It was so nice to dress in jeans and relax right there beside the ocean!

We look forward to repaying your hospitality some day when you schedule a visit to our offices.

Sincerely,

[Your Name]
[Your Address, if not on letterhead]

Thank-You Letter to Employee

[Date]

[Name]
[Address]
[City, State ZIP]

Dear [Mr./Ms. Last Name]:

Thank you so much for going well beyond the call of duty in completing the [Name] project. You clearly understood how important this project is to the company. I appreciate your efforts.

The client is very satisfied with our work, and I know it is due in great deal to all of your diligence. You showed great team leadership and an ability to prioritize and implement a plan.

Thank you again for your efforts!

Sincerely,

[Your Name]
[Your Address, if not on letterhead]

If you work closely with this employee, the salutation would, of course, be his or her first name. Employees can put letters like this in their file for future use, not necessarily just for a new job but for things like applying for scholarships or other programs. And even if they never use it for anything else, it is nice to be appreciated.

Letter Requesting Permission

Publishers will often have their own permission agreements that you will have to use when securing permissions. Your cover letter can introduce the project without the burden of the contract legalese and outline the key points in the contract.

[Date]

[Name]
[Address]
[City, State ZIP]

Dear [Mr./Ms. Last Name]:

I am writing a book called [Book Title] and would like permission to use your photograph, [Photo Title], which I saw on your Web site.

The book is being published by [Publisher Name] and is scheduled for [Month] [Year] publication. The first printing will be [Hard Cover/Paperback] of approximately [Number]. I am requesting nonexclusive North American rights.

In compensation, I can pay [Amount] and [Number] copies of the book.

If this is agreeable to you, please review sign the attached contract. If you have any further questions, I would be happy to answer them. You can reach me at the number listed below.

Sincerely,

[Your Name]
[Your Address, if not on letterhead]

Letter Requesting Permission

[Date]

[Name]
[Address]
[City, State ZIP]

Dear [Mr./Ms. Last Name]:

My company, [Company Name], is planning an employee appreciation day at our property on [Road] on [Date]. We would like to include a short hike as part of our activities that day; the hike we have mapped out would take us across your field.

Would it be OK for us to do that? There will be approximately 30 people. We would be certain to not litter or otherwise disturb the field; I understand you cut that field for hay and we could be sure to keep to the stonewall border.

If this is OK with you, I would appreciate it if you could sign this letter and return it to me in the enclosed self-addressed, stamped envelope. That way I can put it in the file for the outing. If you have any questions, you can reach me at [Phone Number] or e-mail me at [E-Mail Address].

Sincerely,

[Your Name]
[Your Address, if not on letterhead]

This is another matter that it might seem at first could be handled in a phone call. However, it is always best to have any permissions granted in writing and on file. And you would want to bring a copy of the signed letter on the hike in case anyone questioned you.

## Chapter 16

International Letters

Business transactions with companies in other parts of the world are a common practice today. In the 1800s sailing ships brought supplies, months of letters and newspapers, and political announcements to other parts of the world. Traders and businessmen sought ways to obtain the news "off the boat" before their competitors, so that they could buy or sell products, raise prices, or reduce losses before the news was common knowledge.

Our ability to access information and communicate it to a global audience has evolved, especially as technology has become a tool that all businesses can utilize. Our ability to communicate information, while global, requires that consideration be given to two key factors: what message is being communicated, and who will be on the receiving end of the message.

You Say "Potato," I Say "Potahto"....

Problems dealing with international customers or vendors frequently are the result of poor communication. Imagine that you are a customer in another part of the world and you have contacted a business in the U.S. to place an order. The person in the U.S., trying to reassure his client that this kind of request is "all in a day's work" has just implied that whatever the client wants, it will be available in a single work day. Yikes! Using an expression common to Americans has created an "instant disconnect" between expectation and ability—and both parties are speaking English!

Literal translation from one language to another can also cause problems. A common story that illustrates this point is that of General Motors and their Latin American advertising campaign for the Chevrolet Nova. If only one person had realized that the literal translation of "No Va" to Spanish is "No Go," General Motors might have named this automobile something different—at least for its Spanish-speaking customers!

Noting that someone has made an error is hard to do in any language! While it's important to say that you feel an error has been made, the "niceties" of International Business suggest that whenever possible, you should not place any blame, just make a someone generic inquiry so that the person on the other end can save face.

Idioms

The dictionary defines the word "idiom" as "A style or manner of expression peculiar to a given people." When do you use an idiom when composing an international letter? Never! Translation is often literal, and can create a situation ranging from confusion to insult. Here are just a few of our favorite expressions that can be found in business letters, expressions that, when translated literally, don't express what we intend to express:

- By the way
- Bare bones
- Cutthroat
- Flooding the market
- Explore every avenue
- Lame excuse
- Pet name
- Priced out of the market
- Sharp tongued
- Splitting hairs

Avoid these and any other idioms and clichés you can think of. Read your letters carefully to pick them out and rephrase them with very general language, such as changing "we will explore every avenue" to "we will look into every possible way of doing this job."

Keep It Simple

Americans have become sloppy in writing letters, using acronyms, slang expressions, and minimal punctuation. Americans also tend to be less formal in their communication with one another. When composing a letter to someone in another country however, it's often helpful to go back to the "old rules" for ^punctuation.

When communicating to a global audience, the best way to get your point across, and earn the appreciation of your recipient, is to present the information in a format that is easy to read and understand. The preceding sentence for example, may have too many commas for the American audience but is a good example of breaking a sentence down for non-native English speakers/readers so that the message is given in blocks. Short declarative statements are easier to translate and keep the reader focused on the message, rather than the vocabulary. Inserting commas and semicolons will help the reader understand when to pause.

It's also a common American practice to note a nonspecific statement by bracketing it in quote marks. This is not done in other countries, and will confuse the reader. Requesting specific information in your correspondence will produce a better result. Asking for a delivery "in early spring" is too ambiguous. Are you asking for a delivery when its spring for you, or when its spring in the country you are ordering from?

Some Formatting Details

International letters tend to use the full block format or the block format. What does this mean?

- In "full-block format" all the elements of the letter begin flush left.
- In "block format" means that the date, reference line, closing and signature block are to the right of the center of the page
- "Modified block" is not often used in international correspondence. It is similar to the block format except paragraphs are indented.

If you or your company compose International correspondence frequently, it's better to standardize your letter type. Not only can you create a template but also having all your correspondence look the same will help to minimize confusion.

Lastly, dates should always be spelled out to avoid confusion. For example, write May 3, 2005 not 5/3/2005. Using 5/3/2005 means May 3rd to you and me, but to many other people, including the English-speaking United Kingdom, it would mean the 5th of March.

Salutation

Forms of address vary all over the world and we could devote an entire chapter to listing how to address letters, by country. A quick rule of thumb is to keep it formal, address your letter using either Mr. or Mrs. (Ms is not as common in letters coming from other countries) or a title, if one has been given. Keep the same format in your salutation. The use of first names is common in the United States but can be considered too informal, or even cause offense by being "overly familiar" in some parts of the world. When you have received a letter from someone who has addressed you formally, return the courtesy. When in doubt, ask! When you address a letter to an unrelated man and woman, use both their names and in the inside address, and salutation, for example:

Mr. John Doe
Mrs. Jane Smith
[Company Name]
[Address]
[City, State, Zip]
Dear Mr. Doe and Mrs. Smith:

In Asian cultures the last name is typically first. Therefore, a letter addressed to Mr. Toshihito Hata would begin with the salutation, "Dear Mr. Toshihito." Japanese will often address one another as "san." "Toshihito San" is a respectful and less formal way to speak to Mr.

Toshihito, but not in your initial letter! That form of address is better used once a relationship has developed, and then carefully and in the right circumstances.

The way your letters close is also an important component and over-familiarity can create problems. "With warm regards," something we see frequently in letters in the U.S., is considered too personal in many parts of the world. "Sincerely" or "Regards" is often used when communicating with someone for the first time. When the letter is sent by a woman, Mrs., Miss, or Ms., appears in parentheses before the first and last name in the signature block. Mr. does not appear in parentheses.

If you are replying to a letter in which the writer has identified themselves as Professor Smith, address him that way in your response. In some parts of the world having a college degree (bachelor's and higher) means that they are addressed using a title. The title can vary depending on the country, and the field that person is in. Watch for it and use it—this small courtesy will go a long way toward opening a cordial and successful relationship.

The Soft Sell

Good manners are an important part of all correspondence, and again there is a significant cultural difference between countries in how questions are asked, information is given, and conflicts are resolved. The tone of a letter is as important as the way it's worded and will have an impact in how quickly and how satisfactorily the business is handled. Americans would think nothing of sending a "demand for payment" letter worded:

"Full payment of the past due invoice is expected within 1ays, or other action will be taken."

Writing a more carefully worded past due invoice to someone overseas would yield a better result:

"We would appreciate your attention to this matter, and would like to hear from you concerning this misplaced invoice within 10 days, if possible."

Everyone knows the invoice isn't missing, it's just not paid, but asking for payment, rather than demanding it, allows the recipient to save face, and take care of the matter promptly.

English is considered to be the universal language of business, but we must not forget it's not the only language in the world. Taking some time to understand the business practices, culture, and niceties of doing business in another county will give you an advantage over those who compete for business as though they were in their own backyard.

Letter Arranging Visit

This letter is very brief and to the point. It acknowledges previous correspondence, gives a brief outline for the purpose of the visit and suggests a potential outcome. Note the writer is clearly stating gender and that they are both meeting with the recipient. This letter is in a full block format.

[Date]

[Reference]

[Name and Title]
[Company Name]
[Address]
[City, Province, Country, Post Code]

Dear [Mr./Mrs. Last Name]:

Thank you for your invitation to visit your factory on September 20 and 21, 2006.

Mr. [Name] and I accept your invitation to see your manufacturing plant and learn more about your product. [Company Name] is well known in the United States for the quality and durability of your electronics and we will be pleased to discuss possible distribution agreements with you, after our tour.

We will contact you once our travel arrangements have been finalized. We look forward to meeting you.

Sincerely yours,

[Name]
[Title]

Thank-You Letter for Visit

[Date]

[Reference]

[Name and Title]
[Company Name]
[Address]
[City, Province, Country, Post Code]

Dear [Mr./Mrs. Last Name]:

Thank you for the courtesy you extended while [Mr./Ms. Name] and I were visiting recently. When [Mr./Ms. Name] guided us on a tour of your plant, we were thoroughly impressed. We saw a cost-efficient and modern operation. We were particularly impressed with the procedures you have implemented to monitor quality control.

All of your employees were extremely courteous and carefully explained various functions and answered all of our inquiries. The pride they took in their job was evident in their attitude, and in the quality of the finished products.

We will meet with our Management Team next week to discuss our trip, and our discussion with you about distribution of your products in the United States. We expect to have any contract changes to you within 10 days.

Please thank your staff for all the courtesy extended to us. We look forward to speaking with you again soon.

Sincerely,

[Name]
[Title]

The sentences in this letter are shorter and use fewer descriptive adjectives than we might use in a letter to a business professional in this country. Whether the recipient of this letter is fluent in English or uses a translator, eliminating idioms and keeping phrasing clean will help make it easier to understand the content.

Checking on Quote

[Date]

[Reference]

[Name and Title]
[Company Name]
[Address]
[City, Province, Country, Post Code]

Dear [Mr./Mrs. Last Name]:

Thank you for your letter and your quote [Reference] of [Date]. The quantity of electronic components and the delivery schedule you have given us is will meet our requirements.

We wonder if the amount you have quoted for delivery, $16,465, was actually intended to read $1,646.50, which is the total listed on the quote from the shipping company.

If the figure $16,465 is in error, please provide us with an adjusted quote so that we can finalize our purchase order.

Thank you in advance for your assistance.

Sincerely Yours,

[Name]
[Title]

Sending Product Information

[Date]

[Recipient Name]
[Company Name]
[Address]
[City, Province, Country, Post Code]

Dear [Mr./Mrs./Ms. Last Name]:

Thank you for requesting additional information on our [Product]. A brochure that explains how our system operates is enclosed. These components can be combined in a variety of patterns to meet your individual needs. Once you have evaluated the various products, I would be happy to provide you with a quote based on the modules you feel would be best suited to your environment.

I hope that the enclosed information will help you evaluate how our [Product] can exceed your expectations. I appreciate your interest and look forward to hearing from you.

Sincerely,

[Name]
[Title if applicable]

It is always helpful to include a cover letter with any brochure or sales material you send to someone.

Sending Training Manual

[Date]

[Recipient Name]
[Company Name]
[Address]
[City, Province, Country, Post Code]

Dear [Mr./Mrs./Ms. Last Name]:

Here is the information you requested on [product or service]. The enclosed training manual will also provide you with some helpful guidelines for selling this product to your customers.

The process for obtaining a license to import [Product] are fairly strict, and you should consult your solicitor or agent to assure that you can meet each requirement. Once you have ascertained that you are able to secure the licenses needed, we can discuss in more detail what you will need for an initial investment.

I wish you all success in obtaining the required licenses. Please let me know if I can be of additional help.

Sincerely,

[Name]
[Title, if applicable]

Cover letters can provide the opportunity to point out one more time some critical phase that needs to be addressed—such as licenses here—even if you already pointed it out in a phone conversation.

Credit Approval

[Date]

[Recipient Name]
[Company Name]
[Address]
[City, Province, Country, Post Code]

Dear [Mr./Mrs./Ms. Last Name]:

Congratulations! Your company's request for credit has been approved and a new account has been opened in the name of [Company Name].

Please take a moment to familiarize yourself with our terms and conditions, as they apply to your account. If you have any questions or concerns, please let me know, and I will be happy to clarify the details.

The credit representative who will handle your account is [Name] and I am including [His/Her] contact information for your convenience. I know that [Name] will be happy to help you.

Thank you for choosing [Company Name] as your supplier. We look forward to working with you.

Sincerely,

[Name]
[Title, if applicable]

Credit applications and terms apply to foreign accounts as well. Sometimes it is best to give them a little extra payment time just to account for money exchange and customs, etc., but the current state of electronic bank transfers and other technological advances make it easy to do busy overseas.

Request for Overdue Payment

Keep close tabs on account delinquency with international customers. Written notices allow you to keep track of your correspondence and payment requests.

[Date]

[Recipient Name]
[Company Name]
[Address]
[City, Province, Country, Post Code]

Dear [Mr./Mrs./Ms. Last Name]:

Thank you for your order of [Date]. We are pleased that you were able to offer our products to your customer base. I noticed that your initial invoice is now more than 45 days past due. Since we discussed our payment terms during our meeting, I'm sure this is an oversight, and have included a copy of your invoice for your convenience.

Thank you for your attention to this, and please let me know if I can be of assistance.

Sincerely,

[Name]
[Title, if applicable]

Notification of Payment Error

[Date]

[Recipient Name]
[Company Name]
[Address]
[City, Province, Country, Post Code]

Dear [Mr./Mrs./Ms. Last Name]:

Thank you for your prompt payment in the amount of [Amount]. The full amount has been applied to your invoice No. [Number]. I am wondering if there was a typographical error when the check was printed: the dollar figures and the cent figures are reversed from the invoice. The invoice is for "$78.43" and your check is for "$43.78." I am including a copy of the invoice, as well as a copy of your check, so that you can review it with your payables staff.

Please let me know if you need any additional information, as my associates and I are at your service.

Sincerely,

[Name]
[Title, if applicable]

Deal immediately with mistakes in payment like this. The longer they sit, the harder it is to explain them.

Request for Information

[Date]

[Recipient Name]
[Company Name]
[Address]
[City, Province, Country, Post Code]

Dear [Mr./Mrs./Ms. Last Name]:

Please send me information about selecting a site in your country for our business.

[Company Name] is interested in locating a site suitable for a distribution center which will process and ship all orders going to our International Customers. We are interested in an arrangement that would allow us to lease space, with the option to purchase. Details about the size, location preference, and number of anticipated employees are enclosed.

As we evaluate locations for this business, we must know if the following are available, and, if so, what costs are associated with each of them.

- Transportation by ground and air methods
- Warehouse space
- Utilities and other associated overhead costs
- Housing and schools for employees and their families.

We would like to receive this information no later than [date] so that we can plan our visits accordingly. Thank you for your help.

Sincerely,

[Name]
[Title, if applicable]

Requesting information like this via letter allows the recipient to have all the pertinent information in writing, including things like your address. If you called to get the information, you may be trying to give your address to a non-native English speaker.

Requesting Import Information

[Date]

[Recipient Name]
[Company Name]
[Address]

[City, Province, Country, Post Code]

Dear [Mr./Mrs./Ms. Last Name]:

I would like to learn more about the opportunities for becoming an importer of your [Product]. My company, [Company Name], is the premier importer for [Product] and we feel that expanding our line of products to include [product name] will provide a wider range of [equipment/accessories] to our existing customers as well as attract new prospects.

Please provide me with information concerning your price scale, minimums, if required, terms and conditions and any information on duties and taxes. As I have not done business with your country before, I would appreciate any recommendation you may have for brokers and air cargo expeditors.

A brochure with information regarding our company and current product line is included. I look forward to hearing from you at your earliest convenience.

Sincerely,

[Name]
[Title, if applicable]

You will need to send information eventually if you are requesting to import, so you might as well do it upfront with an introductory cover letter.

Requesting Tour

Touring international facilities is a great way to get to know the business workings of a foreign country in which you would like to establish your business.

[Date]

[Recipient Name]
[Company Name]
[Address]
(City, Province, Country, Post Code)

Dear [Mr./Mrs./Ms. Last Name]:

I hope you will accept this letter as an introduction to you.[Company Name] has been in business since [Year], and [Name] and I will be visiting your country from [Date] through [Date]. We would like to arrange a meeting with you for the purpose of visiting your manufacturing facility. The type of manufacturing process you are using is of particular interest to us, as we hope to use a similar process for our products.

Our agent, [Name], will contact you next week to confirm a more specific date and itinerary for our visit. We look forward to meeting you and learning more about your company, and look forward to your favorable response.

Sincerely,

[Name]
[Title, if applicable]

Introducing Colleague

[Date]

[Recipient Name]
[Company Name]
[Address]
[City, Province, Country, Post Code]

Dear [Mr./Mrs./Ms. Last Name]:

This letter is to introduce my trusted associate [Name], who will be visiting your country for the purpose of meeting our International Suppliers. [Name] has been with our company since [Date] and has recently been promoted to the position of [Title]. [Name] duties include maintaining all contractual agreements with our suppliers, and will be in [Country] during the week of [dates].

I am sure that you will find [Name] to be well versed in the manufacturing processes used in [product] and I am equally confident that he will enjoy the same courtesy you have extended to me, during my visits.

[Name] will contact you to make appointment arrangements. We value our relationship with [Company] and look forward to a continued partnership.

Sincerely,

[Name]
[Title, if applicable]

A letter from you introducing a colleague who will be visiting the country and companies there with which you do business is very much international etiquette.

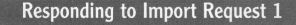

Responding to Import Request 1

[Date]

[Recipient Name]
[Company Name]
[Address]
[City, Province, Country, Post Code]

Dear [Mr./Mrs./Ms. Last Name]:

Thank you for your inquiry regarding the products and services we offer. We appreciate your visiting our web site [link] and sending us your feedback.

We do not have a program for customers outside of the United States at this time. The nature of our product is specific to US regulatory guidelines and has not been modified for an International Market.

There is a possibility that we will develop a similar product that will meet the standards of [Country] in the future, and we will gladly keep your inquiry on file for this possibility.

We regret that we cannot help you in this instance but we value the confidence you place in our product, through your inquiry.

Sincerely,

[Name]
[Title, if applicable]

Sometimes you have to say no, but it is good business to always leave a door open for future possibilities.

Response to Import Request 2

[Date]

[Recipient Name]
[Company Name]
[Address]
[City, Province, Country, Post Code]

Dear [Mr./Mrs./Ms. Last Name]:

Thank you for your phone call today and your interest in distributing [product] in [Country]. The options for purchasing our product internationally have been somewhat limited, and my partners and I are would like to explore this opportunity with you in more detail.

Each of the distributors currently working with our company are operating as independent channel partners, and have been able to offer our products at a competitive price, because the options for [product] have been limited outside of the United States.

Your cost will vary depending on the range of products and quantities you select, but I have included a price list to give you an idea of the cost/sell ratio. Typically our distributors have pre-paid freight and added on to their customer invoices, and while you have other duties and import fees to consider, you may be able to institute a similar arrangement in your country.

Once you have reviewed the pricing, and contracts please call or email me so that we can discuss them in detail. I look forward to speaking with you again, and working with you in the future.

Sincerely,

[Name]
[Title, if applicable]

A letter about potential foreign distribution can provide information on pricing and other details that the potential distributor can keep on file for future reference. Plus having this kind of information in a written letter allows you to keep track of what you told the distributor.

Thank-you Letter

[Date]

[Recipient Name]
[Company Name]
[Address]
[City, Province, Country, Post Code]

Dear [Mr./Mrs./Ms. Last Name]:

Thank you for all the courtesies you extended me during my recent visit to your country. I was delighted with the sites you selected as possible manufacturing and warehousing locations, and will evaluate all the data you thoughtfully provided.

I will not soon forget my first visit to [name of country], and hope that this visit was one of many to come, as we develop our relationship with your country and its citizens.

Sincerely,

[Name]
[Title, if applicable]

Never forget to send a thank-you letter!

Response to Receipt of Materials

[Date]

[Recipient Name]
[Company Name]
[Address]
[City, Province, Country, Post Code]

Dear [Mr./Mrs./Ms. Last Name]:

Thank you for responding to my inquiry so promptly. I have reviewed the catalog and ordering information that you provided, as well as the terms and conditions for importation of [Product] to my country.

I have forwarded the contracts to my Attorney and expect to meet with him early next week. I will be in touch with you later next week with any questions or comments he might have. I expect that we will reply favorably to your offer, and look forward to speaking with you soon.

Sincerely,

[Name]
[Title, if applicable]

Always follow up on receipt of materials and outline what steps you are taking next.

Thank-you for Samples

When a company takes the time and incurs the cost to send sample products for your review, be sure to send a letter acknowledging their receipt and what your plans are.

[Date]

[Recipient Name]
[Company Name]
[Address]
[City, Province, Country, Post Code]

Dear [Mr./Mrs./Ms. Last Name]:

Thank you for sending me the samples of [product] for evaluation. I have forwarded them to our Vice President of Marketing for her input.

I was pleased with the quality and workmanship and would like to consider including these items in our Winter/Holiday catalog. I am including a sales projection, and would appreciate a price quote based on the total projection in one order, as well as the total projection purchased in three equal shipments.

Once I have reviewed the pricing, I will be in touch with you within a week to finalize our agreement. I look forward to offering my customers the finely crafted products made by [Company Name].

Sincerely,

[Name]
[Title, if applicable]

Check Your
Proofreading Ability!

Each of the letters on the following pages has the accurate version on the left side and the version with mistakes on the right. First, cover over the letter on the left and find any general typos and mistakes you can in the letter on the right. Then, uncover the letter on the left to see how good you are at comparing the two letters to find mistakes. Then to check your proofreading, look at the end to find each letter with the mistakes highlighted.

November 12, 2004

Jason Collier
Anderson Asphalt Company
2169 Jackson Avenue
Biloxi, MS 82364

Dear Mr. Collier,

This is to confirm our conversation of November 10 at the Radisson Hotel conference about scheduling the repaving of our company parking lot. Thanks for accommodating our desire to complete this job during the Christmas week shut-down of our factory. You also thought you could recommend a subcontractor to paint in the lines for parking spaces. I'd appreciate it if you would send me that contact information by return mail, Jason.

Here are the details I promised to send to you. Our parking lot is 200 x 350', for a total of 70,000 square feet. You quoted us a price of $5.50 per square foot, including the removal of existing pavement and preparing the surface for new asphalt. The price we agreed on is $385,000. You agreed that work would begin on December 26, 2004, estimated to be completed in four business days.

If you can confirm the above dates and costs on a contract to be received by us before November 23 and schedule your crews accordingly, we will send you the agreed upon 10% deposit of $38,500 by December 20, 2004. Jackson Ball Bearings looks forward to doing business with you.

Sincerely,

Stuart Jackson, Vice President
Jackson Ball Bearing Company
673 Collier Street
Biloxi, MI 82606

November 12, 2004

Jason Collier
Anderson Asphalt Company
2196 Jackson Avenue
Biloxi, MI 82364

Dear Ms. Collier,

This is to confirm our conversation of November 10 at the Radisson Hotel conference about scheduling the repaving of our company parking lot. Thanks for accommodating our desire to complete this job during the Christmas week shut-down of our factory. You also thought you could recommend a subcontractor to paint in the lines for parking spaces. I'd appreciate it if you would send me that contact information by return mail, John.

Here are the details I promised to send to you. Our parking lot is 200 x 350', for a total of 60,000 square feet. You quoted us a price of $5.50 per square foot, including the removal of existing pavement and preparing the surface for new asphalt. The price we agreed on is $358,000. You agreed that work would begin on December 26, 2004, estimated to be completed in four business days.

If you can confirm the above dates and costs on a contract to be received by us before November 23 and schedule your crews accordingly, we will send you the agreed upon 10% deposit of $58,500 by December 20, 2004. Jackson Ball Bearings looks forward to doing business with you.

Sincerely,

Stewart Jackson, Vice President
Jackson Ball Bearing Company
673 Collier Street
Biloxi, MI 86206

September 8, 2003

Beverly Crawford
Miami Humane Society
3749 Sunset Street
Miami, FL 47261

Dear Ms. Crawford,

Thanks for your phone call last week regarding the purchase of 185 doses of distemper vaccines and 310 units of heartworm medication. We are pleased to inform you that we can accommodate your order at the discount price discussed.

Please sign the attached contract and confirm quantities, prices, and requested shipping dates. Return it to us promptly to reserve your order. Because vaccinations must be refrigerated, please allow an extra three days for the carrier to schedule a shipment.

Our company will also send ten boxes of our new flea preventative with your order at no extra charge. It is our pleasure to support animal shelters in their important work. Thanks for the opportunity to serve you.

Sincerely,

Althea Day
Fido's Healthcare Company
2131 South Harvard Road
Stanhope, OH 57248

September 8, 2003

Beverly Crawford
Miami Humane Society
3947 Sunset Street
Miami, FL 47261

Dear Ms. Crawford,

Thanks for your phone call last week regarding the purchase of 185 doses of distemper vaccines and 210 units of heartworm medication. We are pleased to inform you that we can accommodate your order at the discount price discussed.

Please sign the attached contract and confirm quantities, prices, and requested shipping dates. Return it to us promply to reserve your order. Because vacinations must be refrigerated, please allow an extra three days for the carrier to schedule a shipment.

Our company will also send ten boxes of our new flea preventative with your order at no extra charge. It is our pleasure to support animal shelters in their important work. Thanks for the opportunity to serve you.

Sincerely,

Althea Day
Fido's Healthcare Company
2131 South Harvard Road
Stanhipe, OH 57248

April 23, 2003

Carol Dexter
Nova Services
28 Parkside Drive
Toledo, OH 59732

Dear Ms. Dexter,

I have noticed a discrepancy on the bill we received from your company dated April 19. The amount charged for Sandra Moriarty for two weeks of temporary receptionist services exceeds our contract by $75.

Sandra worked for a total of 60 hours. Our contract states that her hourly rate would be $7.25. However, we were billed at an hourly rate of $8.10, for a total of $510.00. The contracted total was $435.00.

Thanks for checking into this for us, Carol. Upon receipt of a corrected invoice, we will send payment.

Sincerely,

Suki Yoshuru
Accounts Payable
Good Hands Insurance
3438 Tower Way
Emmaus, PA 26743

April 23, 2003

Carol Dexter
Nova Services
29 Parkside Drive
Toledo, OH 59723

Dear Ms. Dexter,

I have noticed a discrepincy on the bill we received from your company dated April 19. The amount charged for Sandra Morirty for two weeks of temporary receptionist services exceeds our contract by $75.

Sandra worked for a total of 60 hours. Our contract states that her hourly rate would be $6.25. However, we were billed at an hourly rate of $8.10, for a total of $510.00. The contracted total was $453.00.

Thanks for checking into this for us, Carol. Upon receipt of a corrected invoice, we will send payment.

Sincerely,

Suki Yoshuri
Accounts Payable
Good Hands Insurance
3483 Tower Way
Emmaus, PA 27643

September 4, 2002

Jose Perez
Peterson's Flooring Emporium
583 Hudson Avenue
Peekskill, NY 12749

Dear Mr. Perez,

Your services were recommended by a friend, Sadie Lamb, who was a customer several years ago. We admired the tile your company provided and installed in her home. We have tried to match it in our local area, without success.

Sadie can't remember just when the work was done, nor does she have the receipt that might give details about ordering the tile. We hope that your records might provide the missing information. We provide Sadie's address and telephone number to help you find her in your files. She is happy to confirm her agreement to this process, if you want to contact her.

> Sadie Lamb
> 37 Elm Street
> La Grange, NY 12643
> (212) 555-3478

If you can identify the tile that went into Sadie's house and had it in stock or could order it, we would love to discuss the details of purchasing it from you. We hope you can help!

Truly yours,

Bob and Linda Grimes
389 Freedom Drive
Farmington, NY 12543

September 4, 2002

Jose Perez
Peterson's Flooring Emporium
583 Hudson Avenue
Peekskill, NY 12749

Dear Mr. Perez,

Your services were recommended by a friend, Sadie Lamb, who was a custemer several years ago. We admired the tile your company provided and installed in her home. We have tried to match it in our local area, without success.

Sadie can't remember just when the work was done, nor does she have the receipt that might give details about ordering the tile. We hope that your records might provide the missing infirmation. We provide Sadie's address and telephone number to help you find her in your files. She is happy to confirm her agreement to this process, if you want to contact her.

> Sadie Jenkins
> 73 Elm Street
> La Grange, NY 12643
> (212) 555-3874

If you can identify the tile that went into Sadie's house and had it in stock or could order it, we would love to discuss the detials of purchasing it from you. We hope you can help!

Truly yours,

Bob and Linda Jenkins
389 Freedom Drive
Farmington, NY 12543

March 11, 1999

Sarah Peavey
Sunny Acres Farm
91 Farm Ridge Road
Blaine, MT 64931

Dear Ms. Peavey,

As you may know, Saddle Up Stables in Blaine are for sale. I am considering buying the property as a boarding and lesson facility. In my long-distance discussions with the current owner, your name was mentioned as a possible source for quality hay.

I anticipate that I would require between 7,200 and 7,400 bales a year. The loft at Saddle Up will hold a month's worth, or about 600 bales. Would your fields provide that amount of hay annually? Would monthly delivery and unloading be possible to arrange?

If the answer is yes to these questions, I'd be happy to speak with you about establishing a relationship. I'll be out of the country until the end of April. Please contact me at the address below to let me know if you are interested. If not, do you know any other local hay producers who might be? Thanks in advance for your time.

Best,

Lonnigan Brady
92 Cambridge Street
Malden, MA 02568

March 11, 1999

Sarah Peevey
Sunny Acres Farm
91 Farm Ridge Road
Blaine, MI 64931

Dear Ms. Peavey,

As you may know, Saddle Up Stables in Blaine are for sale. I am considering buying the property as a baording and lesson facility. In my long-distance discussions with the current owner, your name was mentioned as a possible source for quality hay.

I anticipate that I would require between 7,200 and 8,400 bales a year. The loft at Saddle Up will hold a month's worth, or about 600 bales. Would your feilds provide that amount of hay annualy? Would monthly delivery and unloading be possible arrange?

If the answer is yes to these questions, I'd be happy to speak with you about establishing a relationship. I'll be out of the country until the end of April. Please contact me at the adress below to let me know if you are interested. If not, do you any other local hay producers who might be? Thanks in advance for your time.

Best,

Lonnigan Brody
92 Cambridge Street
Malden, MA 02865

May 2, 1998
Candid Camera Shoppe
Customer Service Department
89 Holly Corner
Granville, IL 34185

Greetings.

In 1989, I purchased a Nikon 35mm SLR camera from you, with a very special telephoto lens made in Denmark, for photographing tiny things. I specialize in Victorian miniatures. The camera took marvelous photographs for 10 years. Sadly, I dropped the lens and cracked it. I'm hoping it can be repaired.

I have inquired in my local area, but no one seems to have access to parts or service for this lens. I'm hoping that you do. It's a Bjorklund 9600, 400mm lens. I'm happy to ship it to you from California, where I now live, if your service team can help. Can you?

Sincerely,

Arthur Toggenburg
236748 Pacific Boulevard
Del Coronado, CA 92618
(673) 845-1989

May 2, 1998
Candid Camera Shop
Customer Srvice Department
89 Holly Corner
Granville, IL 34185

Greetings.

In 1989, I purchased a Nikon 335mm SLR camera from you, with a very special telephoto lens made in Denmark, for photographing tiny things. I specialize in Victorian minitures. The camera took marvelous photographs for 10 years. Sadly, I dropped the lens and cracked it. I'm hoping it can be repired.

I have inquired in my local area, but no one seems to have axxess to parts or service for this lens. I'm hoping that you do. It's a Biorklund 9700, 400mm lens. I'm happy to ship it to you from California, where I now live, if your service teem can help. Can you?

Sincerely,

Arthur Togginberg
236749 Pacific Buolevard
Del Coronado, CA 92618
(674) 845-1998

April 14, 2003

Fins and Shells Seafood Company
ATTN: Marcy Delrio
24 Ocean Blvd.
New Bedford, MA 02634

Dear Ms. Delrio,

We here at the Community Vocational College are excited about the graduation clambake your company has agreed to cater for us on June 7 this year. To confirm our conversation earlier this week, here are the details.

We are expecting 52 graduates and 104 guests, as well as 25 faculty and staff. To feed these 181 people, you advised that we would require:

250 pounds of clams,

250 stuffed quahogs,

200 ears of corn,

100 pounds of potato salad,

75 pounds of green salad,

25 pounds of Indian pudding,

and 50 pounds of vanilla ice cream.

Your company will also provide soft drinks, bottled water, coffee and tea for the gathering. Your staff will arrive at 10AM on June 7 to set up the food in time for the 2PM clambake. The bake pit will have been dug for your staff in advance. By 5PM that day, your staff will have completed the clean-up.

We will send a deposit of $2,354, half the contracted price, upon receipt of a written contract from Fins and Shells.

Thanks in advance for your excellent service and food.

Sincerely,

Barbara Jones
Events Coordinator
CVC
3472 Fairhaven Rd.
Fall River, MA 02573

April 14, 2003

Fins and Shells Seafood Company
ATTN: Marc Delrio
24 Ocean Blvd.
New Bedford, MA 02634

Dear Mr. Delrio,

We here at the Community Vocationl College are excited about the graduation lambake your company has agreed to cater for us on June 6 this year. To confirm our conversation earlier this week, here are the details.

We are expecting 52 graduates and 401 guests, as well as 25 faclty and staff. To feed these 131 people, you advised that we would require:

250 pounds of clams,

250 stuffed quahogs,

200 ears of corn,

100 pounds of potatoe salad,

25 pounds of green salad,

75 pounds of Indian pudding,

and 50 pounds of vanilla ice cream.

Your company will also provide soft drinks, bttled water, coffee and tea for the gathering. Your staff will arrive at 10AM on June 9 to set up the food in time for the 2AM clambake. The bake pit will have been dug for your staff in advance. By 5PM that day, your staff will have completed the clean-up.

We will send a deposit of $2,534, half the contracted price, upon receipt of a written contract from Fins and Smells.

Thanks in advance for your excellent service and food.

Sincerely,

Barbara Jones
Events Coordinater
CVC
3472 Fairhaven Rd.
Fall River, MA 02573

September 8, 2004

Basil Rathbone
Good Times Marina
459 Ocean Way
Camden, ME 04582

Dear Mr. Rathbone,

Thanks for your interest in our de-icing system. Free Docks offers a patented system that guarantees the end of docks damaged by winter ice and spring ice thaw. We have installed several systems for your neighbors in Maine. I've enclosed a list of a few satisfied customers who have agreed to show you their systems, if you are interested.

You requested our price guidelines. For basic installation, which includes all hardware, our fee is $23.50 per square foot. Each dock requires installations on each side. A typical 12-foot dock, therefore, costs about $564 to keep free from ice damage forever. I'm sure you'll agree that the benefits exceed this low price.

Please call us to discuss details. It will be our pleasure to answer any questions or arrange a meeting at your marina to discuss your particular situation.

Sincerely,

Scott Admiral
Free Docks Enterprises
49247 Falmouth Road
Yarmouth, ME 04921
Encl

September 8, 2004

Basil Rathbone
Good Times Marina
4480cean Way
Camden, ME 05482

Dear Mr. Rathbone,

Thanks for your interest in our de-icing system. Free Ducks offers a patented system that guarantees the end of docks damaged by winter ice and spring ice thaw. We have installed several systems for your neighbors in Maine. I've enclosed a list of a few satisfeid customers who have agreed to show you their systems, if you are interested.

You requested our price guidelines. For basic instullation, which includes all hardware, our fee is $23.50 per square foot. Each dock requires installations on each side. A typical 12-foot dock, therefore, costs about $654 to keep free from ice damage forever. I'm sure you'll agree that the benefits exceed this low price.

Please call us to discuss details. It will be our pleasure to answr any questions or arrange a meeting at your marina to discuss your particular situatin.

Sincerely,

Scott Admiral
Free Docks Enterprises
49247 Falmuoth Road
Yqrmouth, ME 04921
Encl

March 22, 2002

Benjamin Siemens
A-Plus Used Cars
73 Hyland Hill
Springfield, MO 52481

Dear Mr. Siemens,

As part of the disposition of my husband's estate, I have two lightly used vehicles that need to be sold. One is a Ford Explorer, 1999, with 65,450 miles, in perfect condition with lots of extras. The other is a 1998 Cadillac only used to for our winter trips to Florida. It has 45,672 miles and looks brand new. I have enclosed photographs.

I am now residing in Ohio and would like to have these cars sold. Are you interested in purchasing them for resale on your lot? If you would like to see the vehicles and make an offer that includes removing them to your lot, please contact my son, Robert, at 815 947-9002. I am sending this letter to three other dealers in town, so your quick response would be in your favor. I know that friends of my late husband bought good cars from you and that he would appreciate your honest reputation regarding his cars.

Sincerely,

Rita George
Encl:

March 22, 2002

Benjamin Siemens
A-Plus Used Cars
73 Hiland Hill
Springfeild, MO 52481

Dear Mr. Semens,

As part of the disposition of my husband's estate, I have two lightly used vehicles that need to be solded. One is a Ford Explorer, 1999, with 56,450 miles, in perfect condition with lots of extras. The other is a 1998 Cadillac only used to for our winter trips to Florida. It has 45,276 miles and looks brand new. I have enclosed photographs.

I am now residing in Ohio and would like to have these cars sold. Are you interested in purchasing them for reasle on your lot? If you would like to see the vehicls and make an offer that includes remving them to your lot, please contact my son, Robert, at 851 947-9002. I am sending this letter to three other dealers in town, so your quick response would be in your favor. I know that freindof my late husband bought good cars from you and that he would appresiate your honest reputation regarding his cars.

Sincerely,

Rita Peters
Encl:

December 2, 2004

Santini's Towing Service
Tony Santini, Owner
76 Brooklyn Parkway
Rosedale, NY 17382

Dear Mr. Santini,

This letter serves as notice that your loan account is 90 days overdue. If you do not pay off the loan amount on your account #WT908361, for the purchase of a 2003 Chevrolet tow truck, serial number TYP88900334, with a balance remaining of $18,934, by January 4, 2005, repossession processes will be instituted for said vehicle.

Please contact us at your earliest convenience to discuss this matter and advise us of your intentions.

Sincerely,

Robert Antonio
Credit manager
Rosedale Credit Union
1821 Barrington Avenue
Rosedale, NY 17323

December 2, 2004

Santini's Towing Service
Tony Santini, Owner
76 Brooklinn Prkway
Rosedale, NY 17382

Dear Mr. Santini,

This letter serves as notice that your loan account is 90 days overdue. If you do not pay off the loan amount on your account #WT9809361, for the purchase of a 2003 Chevrolet tow truck, serial number TYP88900433, with a balance remaining of $17,834, by January 4, 2005, repossission processes will be instatuted for said vehicle.

Please contact us at your earliest conveneince to discuss this matter and advise us of you intentions.

Sincerely,

Robert Antonio
Credit mnager
Rosedale Credit Union
1821 Barrington Avenue
Rusedale, NY 17232

Letter, Page 244

November 12, 2004

Jason Collier
Anderson Asphalt Company
2196 Jackson Avenue
Biloxi, MS 82364

Dear Ms. Collier,

This is to confirm our conversation of November 10 at the Radisson Hotel conference about scheduling the repaving of our company parking lot. Thanks for accommodating our desire to complete this job during the Christmas week shut-down of our factory. You also thought you could recommend a subcontractor to paint in the lines for parking spaces. I'd appreciate it if you would send me that contact information by return mail, **John**.

Here are the details I promised to send to you. Our parking lot is 200 x 350', for a total of **60**,000 square feet. You quoted us a price of $5.50 per square foot, including the removal of existing pavement and preparing the surface for new asphalt. The price we agreed on is $**358**,000. You agreed that work would begin on December 26, 2004, estimated to be completed in four business days.

If you can confirm the above dates and costs on a contract to be received by us before November 23 and schedule your crews accordingly, we will send you the agreed upon 10% deposit of $**58**,500 by December 20, 2004. Jackson Ball Bearings looks forward to doing business with you.

Sincerely,

Stewart Jackson, Vice President
Jackson Ball Bearing Company
673 Collier Street
Biloxi, MI **862**06

Letter, Page 245

September 8, 2003

Beverly Crawford
Miami Humane Society
3947 Sunset Street
Miami, FL 47261

Dear Ms. Crawford,

Thanks for your phone call last week regarding the purchase of 185 doses of distemper vaccines and 210 units of heartworm medication. We are pleased to inform you that we can accommodate your order at the discount price discussed.

Please sign the attached contract and confirm quantities, prices, and requested shipping dates. Return it to us **promply** to reserve your order. Because **vacinations** must be refrigerated, please allow an extra three days for the carrier to schedule a shipment.

Our company will also send ten boxes of our new flea preventative with your order at no extra charge. It is our pleasure to support animal shelters in their important work. Thanks for the opportunity to serve you.

Sincerely,

Althea Day
Fido's Healthcare Company
2131 South Harvard Road
Stanhipe, OH 57248

Letter, Page 246

April 23, 2003

Carol Dexter
Nova Services
29 Parkside Drive
Toledo, OH 59723

Dear Ms. Dexter,

I have noticed a discrepincy on the bill we received from your company dated April 19. The amount charged for Sandra **Morirty** for two weeks of temporary receptionist services exceeds our contract by $75.

Sandra worked for a total of 60 hours. Our contract states that her hourly rate would be $6.25. However, we were billed at an hourly rate of $8.10, for a total of $510.00. The contracted total was $453.00.

Thanks for checking into this for us, Carol. Upon receipt of a corrected invoice, we will send payment.

Sincerely,

Suki Yoshuri
Accounts Payable
Good Hands Insurance
3483 Tower Way
Emmaus, PA 27643

Letter, Page 247

September 4, 2002

Jose Perez
Peterson's Flooring Emporium
583 Hudson Avenue
Peekskill, NY 12749

Dear Mr. Perez,

Your services were recommended by a friend, Sadie Lamb, who was a **custemer** several years ago. We admired the tile your company provided and installed in her home. We have tried to match it in our local area, without success.

Sadie can't remember just when the work was done, nor does she have the receipt that might give details about ordering the tile. We hope that your records might provide the missing **infirmation**. We provide Sadie's address and telephone number to help you find her in your files. She is happy to confirm her agreement to this process, if you want to contact her.

> Sadie **Jenkins**
> **73** Elm Street
> La Grange, NY 12643
> (212) 555-3**874**

If you can identify the tile that went into Sadie's house and had it in stock or could order it, we would love to discuss the det**ia**ls of purchasing it from you. We hope you can help!

Truly yours,

Bob and Linda **Jenkins**
389 Freedom Drive
Farmington, NY 12543

Letter, Page 248

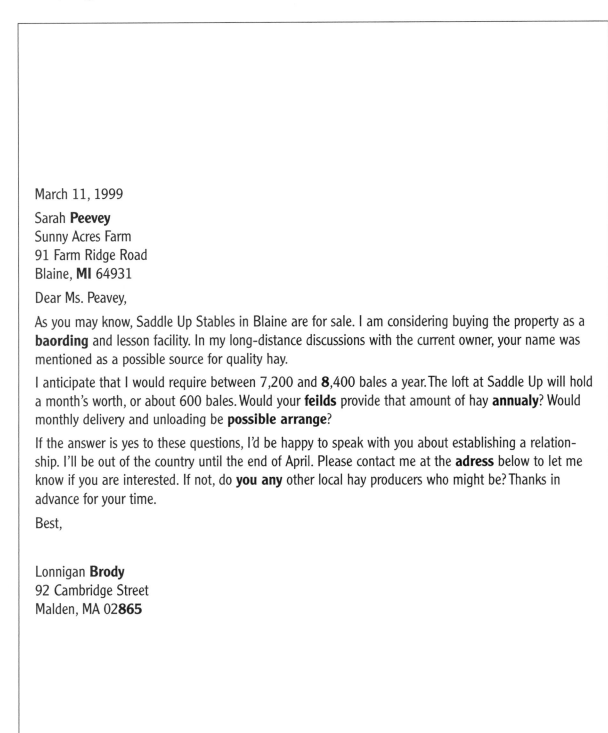

March 11, 1999

Sarah **Peevey**
Sunny Acres Farm
91 Farm Ridge Road
Blaine, **MI** 64931

Dear Ms. Peavey,

As you may know, Saddle Up Stables in Blaine are for sale. I am considering buying the property as a **baording** and lesson facility. In my long-distance discussions with the current owner, your name was mentioned as a possible source for quality hay.

I anticipate that I would require between 7,200 and **8**,400 bales a year. The loft at Saddle Up will hold a month's worth, or about 600 bales. Would your **feilds** provide that amount of hay **annualy**? Would monthly delivery and unloading be **possible arrange**?

If the answer is yes to these questions, I'd be happy to speak with you about establishing a relationship. I'll be out of the country until the end of April. Please contact me at the **adress** below to let me know if you are interested. If not, do **you any** other local hay producers who might be? Thanks in advance for your time.

Best,

Lonnigan **Brody**
92 Cambridge Street
Malden, MA 02**865**

Letter, Page 249

May 2, 1998

Candid Camera **Shop**
Customer **Srvice** Department
89 Holly Corner
Granville, IL 34185

Greetings.

In 1989, I purchased a Nikon 335mm SLR camera from you, with a very special telephoto lens made in Denmark, for photographing tiny things. I specialize in Victorian **minitures**. The camera took marvelous photographs for 10 years. Sadly, I dropped the lens and cracked it. I'm hoping it can be **repired**.

I have inquired in my local area, but no one seems to have **axxess** to parts or service for this lens. I'm hoping that you do. It's a **Biorklund 9700**, 400mm lens. I'm happy to ship it to you from California, where I now live, if your service t**eem** can help. Can you?

Sincerely,

Arthur **Togginberg**
236749 Pacific **Buolevard**
Del Coronado, CA 92618
(67**4**) 845-19**98**

Letter, Page 250

April 14, 2003

Fins and Shells Seafood Company
ATTN: **Marc** Delrio
24 Ocean Blvd.
New Bedford, MA 02634

Dear Mr. Delrio,

We here at the Community **Vocationl** College are excited about the graduation **lambake** your company has agreed to cater for us on June **6** this year. To confirm our conversation earlier this week, here are the details.

We are expecting 52 graduates and **401** guests, as well as 25 **faclty** and staff. To feed these **131** people, you advised that we would require:

250 pounds of clams,

250 stuffed quahogs,

200 ears of corn,

100 pounds of potatoe salad,

25 pounds of green salad,

75pounds of Indian pudding,

and 50 pounds of vanilla ice cream.

Your company will also provide soft drinks, **bttled** water, coffee and tea for the gathering. Your staff will arrive at 10AM on June **9** to set up the food in time for the 2**AM** clambake. The bake pit will have been dug for your staff in advance. By 5PM that day, your staff will have completed the clean-up.

We will send a deposit of $2,**53**4, half the contracted price, upon receipt of a written contract from Fins and **Sm**ells.

Thanks in advance for your excellent service and food.

Sincerely,

Barbara Jones
Events **Coordinater**
CVC
3472 Fairhaven Rd.
Fall River, MA 02573

Letter, Page 251

September 8, 2004

Basil Rathbone
Good Times Marina
4480cean Way
Camden, ME 05482

Dear Mr. Rathbone,

Thanks for your interest in our de-icing system. Free **Ducks** offers a patented system that guarantees the end of docks damaged by winter ice and spring ice thaw. We have installed several systems for your neighbors in Maine. I've enclosed a list of a few **satisfeid** customers who have agreed to show you their systems, if you are interested.

You requested our price guidelines. For basic **instullation**, which includes all hardware, our fee is $23.50 per square foot. Each dock requires installations on each side. A typical 12-foot dock, there-fore, costs about **$65**4 to keep free from ice damage forever. I'm sure you'll agree that the benefits exceed this low price.

Please call us to discuss details. It will be our pleasure to **answr** any questions or arrange a meeting at your marina to discuss your particular **situatin**.

Sincerely,

Scott Admiral
Free Docks Enterprises
49247 Falm**uo**th Road
Yqrmouth, ME 04921
Encl

Letter, Page 252

March 22, 2002

Benjamin Siemens
A-Plus Used Cars
73 **Hiland** Hill
Springfeild, MO 52481

Dear Mr. **Semens**,

As part of the disposition of my husband's estate, I have two lightly used vehicles that need to be **solded**. One is a Ford Explorer, 1999, with **56**,450 miles, in perfect condition with lots of extras. The other is a 1998 Cadillac only used to for our winter trips to Florida. It has 45,**276** miles and looks brand new. I have enclosed photographs.

I am now residing in Ohio and would like to have these cars sold. Are you interested in purchasing them for **reasle** on your lot? If you would like to see the **vehicls** and make an offer that includes **remving** them to your lot, please contact my son, Robert, at **851** 947-9002. I am sending this letter to three other dealers in town, so your quick response would be in your favor. I know that **freindof** my late husband bought good cars from you and that he would **appresiate** your honest reputation regarding his cars.

Sincerely,

Rita **Peters**
Encl:

Letter, Page 253

December 2, 2004

Santini's Towing Service
Tony Santini, Owner
76 **Brooklinn Prkway**
Rosedale, NY 17382

Dear Mr. Santini,

This letter serves as notice that your loan account is 90 days overdue. If you do not pay off the loan amount on your account #**WT9809361**, for the purchase of a 2003 Chevrolet tow truck, serial number TYP88900433, with a balance remaining of **$17,834**, by January 4, 2005, **repossission** processes will be **instatuted** for said vehicle.

Please contact us at your earliest **conveneince** to discuss this matter and advise us of **you** intentions.

Sincerely,

Robert Antonio
Credit **mnager**
Rosedale Credit Union
1821 Barrington Avenue
Rusedale, NY 17232